Selected praise for Lorna Goodison
From Harvey River

'[A] captivating memoir … Being introduced to the cast
of *From Harvey River* is like sitting down at the family
dining table. You'll stay for the day and then on into the
evening as each new character pulls up a chair.
You could not be in better company.'

New York Times Book Review

'Luminous … Beautiful is the life Goodison evokes from the
far-distant past: Jamaica as paradise … This is Goodison's
tribute to her mother, but more than that, it is a window that
opens on to a society that most of us will never know.'

Washington Post

'Goodison makes lyrical exposition sing with dulcet island
patois in this homage to her mother … Richly textured …
Steeped in local lore and spiced with infectious dialect
and ditties, Goodison's memoir reaches back over
generations to evoke the mythic power of childhood,
the magnetic tug of home and the friction between desire
and duty that gives life its unexpected jolts.'

Publishers Weekly

'Goodison unveils intimate worlds teeming with all the
local flavor and poignancy of a Zora Neale Hurston
novel … A tender, thoughtful portrait of four generations,
prompting hopes that the author's first full-length
prose work won't be her last.'

Kirkus Reviews

'Goodison understands that life struggles are inevitably and inveterately struggles of history as well as struggles of language to memorialize everyday or extraordinary realities and dreams. Goodison's prose creates memorable characters ... and captures them at memorable moments, managing to remain intimate while simultaneously expanding the family history into a mythology of a distinct place and time ...'

Globe and Mail

'Lorna Goodison delivers a memoir so exquisite it stands as an example of the possibilities of the form ... A feat of history, imagination and artistic achievement ...
[It] is a sumptuous montage of landscapes, portraits and anecdotes— sepia-toned period pieces—that impress vividly upon the mind ... Goodison's voice, her tone and choice of language, brilliantly reflects the mingling of African and British culture ... to bring the memoir into the tradition of Edwardian letters, and to bring a marginalized time and place into the mainstream of world history.'

Toronto Star

Redemption Ground

Lorna Goodison

First published in 2018 by
Myriad Editions
www.myriadeditions.com

Myriad Editions
An imprint of New Internationalist Publications
The Old Music Hall, 106–108 Cowley Rd, Oxford OX4 1JE

A CIP catalogue record for this book
is available from the British Library

ISBN (pbk):978-1-912408-13-9
ISBN (ebk): 978-1-912408-14-6

Designed and typeset in Palatino
by WatchWord Editorial Services, London

Printed and bound in Great Britain
by Clays Ltd, St Ives plc

In memory of my sister
Carmen Rose Goodison

and to
Ellen Seligman

Contents

1

'The Song of the Banana Man'
and 'The Fiddler of Dooney'

ONE DAY IN the spring of 1972, my friend Helen and I found ourselves in the city of London, walking along Marylebone High Street. After a few minutes we spotted up ahead of us two policemen proceeding at a slow and stately pace, surveying everything around them as they went. We were young and swift of gait, we soon overtook the two coppers, and as we passed them we noticed one of the 'bobbies', as the Brits used to call them, pointing to a clean, brightly painted tea shop which he proceeded to refer to as a 'tea 'ole'.

Seriously, my friend and I had been walking along looking for a place to have tea on Marylebone High Street when we overheard a policeman say to this other policeman: 'Whassis then, a new tea 'ole?'

Helen and I were not the kind who would pass up the chance to have tea in an 'ole', so we went in and ordered a pot of tea and two bath buns. We ordered bath buns because we'd been taught about them in history class at St Hugh's High School for Girls in Kingston, Jamaica where the curriculum was then heavy on all things British and European, and we were taught a great deal of British social history, much of it from a tome authored by G. M. Trevelyan, whom I later found out was a big-shot Professor of History at Cambridge University. What I remember most about that textbook was that it came bound in maroon-coloured linen.

Helen and I had been taught a lot about 1066 and all that, the Angles, Saxons and Jutes, Boadicea, the Princes in the Tower, Inigo Jones and Capability Brown, and about the Tudors and Stuarts, including a song that was supposed to have been sung by one of the four Marys who were ladies-in-waiting to Mary Queen of Scots:

*Last night there were four Marys, tonight there'll be
    but three,
There was Mary Seaton, and Mary Beaton, and Mary
    Carmichael and me.*

We were taught about the Gunpowder Plot, Perkin Warbeck and Lambert Simnel (who I found particularly fascinating because, as I understood it, there was a kind of cake, a Simnel cake, that was not named for him), the Industrial Revolution, the spanner-in-the-works Luddites, the Wars of the Roses, O white rose of the House of York and blood red rose of the House of Lancaster, Culloden and Flodden and O, the battle lost at Killiecrankie, and the fact that James I nicknamed the Duke of Buckingham 'Steenie', after St Stephen who was said to have had the face of an angel. We were also told that Charles II was so dark-skinned that he was called 'the Black Boy' and that his dying words were 'Let not poor Nelly starve', this in reference to Nell Gwynne who rose from selling oranges at the theatre to being one of the king's most favoured mistresses and was paid a stipend from the public purse. Miss Kingdon, who was also in charge of what was then one of the best school libraries in Jamaica, encouraged us girls to read the works of writers like Anya Seton, Rosemary Sutcliff and Mary Renault, which further added to our store of esoteric knowledge.

So that day in the tea shop, Helen and I chose to order bath buns which, as we had been taught, were not buns you ate as you bathed, but rather fruity cakes baked with a lump of sugar inside and sprinkled with more sugar on top when they came out of the oven – and, having written that, I cannot resist saying something about how countless Africans were stolen, enslaved, brutalised and sacrificed in order for sugar cane to be cultivated, so that others could have bath buns with sugar within and without. Anyway, in honour of our history teachers Glory Robertson and Ethel Kingdon, Helen and I ordered bath buns, and, because we were both in possession of a great mine of useless information about such things, we touched our knives to the buns when they arrived and declared them Members of the Order of the Bath Bun and ordered them to rise before we proceeded to demolish them.

After a while we noticed three guys sitting at the table next to ours doing what we were doing – telling each other stories and jokes and cracking each other up. The three looked over at us just about the same time we became aware of them, and the alpha male in the group smiled and said: 'Ah, you lovely young ladies are from the West Indies, are you not?'

In my broadest Jamaican accent, I said, 'Ow yu know?'

And he said, 'O, we're from Ireland, and as a young boy

growing up in County Mayo, Sister Fidelia made me drop my pennies in the poor box to assist with the education of the suffering children of the West Indies; and I'd say, from listening to you two charming young ladies, I'd say that my pennies were well spent.'

'Oh yeah, well thank you very much; I myself have bought and paid for many an Irish potato.'

And the next thing you know we were all sitting together and drinking toasts to the colonial experience.

To the penny buns and Union Jacks we gobbled down and lifted up on Empire Day!

To the waves ruled by Britannia!

To we who never, never, never again shall be slaves!

To the Queen and all who sail in her (this from one Irish guy).

To the host of golden goddamn daffodils!

To Ted Heath and his brother Hampstead Heath (from the Irish alpha male).

And a whole lot of stupid things like that.

We also did some singing.

Helen and I sang 'Danny Boy' to prove we were familiar with Irish airs; although many years later I read that the song was written by an Englishman, whose sister-in-law gave him the tune to a traditional Irish air, though now 'Danny Boy' is widely regarded as the most Irish of songs.

In return, the three Irish men sang, in plaintive tones, 'Jamaica Farewell'.

I think the alpha guy really liked Helen because he kept gazing at her soulfully as he crooned about leaving a little girl in Kingston town, and later she said something about his eyes, which meant she'd been checking him out too. After the rendition of 'Jamaica Farewell', the Irish alpha male said, 'Yes indeed, I for one have always felt an especial closeness to the West Indies, not only due to the fact that I relinquished many a shiny penny to assist with the education (he pronounced it 'ed-yoo-kay-shan') of the children of your sunny isles, but even more so because I myself have a friend who owns a banana-ripening room in Peckham.'

Just the sound of those words had us doubling over with laughter. A banana-ripening room in Peckham?

To be honest, at the time I thought he was making this up. But as it turns out, according to my brother, Keith Goodison, who is a great fount of knowledge, there used to be banana-ripening rooms all over England, that is, before NAFTA did serious damage to the Caribbean banana industry. Now almost every banana in the western world comes from the giant Chiquita Dole plantations. That day in 1972, in that 'tea 'ole', we did not know that, over thirty years later, a poet named David Rudder would be moved to write a song called 'The Banana Death Song'. We did not know that the independent banana-growers of the Caribbean would one day experience great difficulty in finding export markets for what they once called 'green gold', as Helen and I gleefully recited 'The Song of the Banana Man':

> *Touris, white man, wiping his face*
> *Met me in Golden Grove market place.*
> *He looked at m'ol' clothes brown wid stain,*
> *An soaked right through wid the Portlan rain,*
> *He cas his eye, turn up his nose*
> *He says: 'You're a beggar man, I suppose?'*
> *He says: 'Boy, get some occupation*
> *be of some value to your nation.'*
> *I said: 'By God and dis big right han*
> *you mus recognise a Banana Man.'*

Up in de hills, where de streams are cool,
An mullet and janga swim in de pool,
I have ten acres of mountain side
An a dainty-foot donkey dat I ride,
Four Gros-Michel an four Lacatan,
Some coconut trees, and some hills of yam,
An I pasture on dat very same lan
Five she-goats and a big black ram
Dat by God and dis big right hand
Is the property of a banana man.

And, even as Helen and I threw ourselves into an impassioned rendition of Evan Jones's great poem, I found myself thinking that the banana man sounded like a cool guy, and I wondered if he needed a wife or a girlfriend to help him farm his ten acres.

Not to be outdone; the Irishmen recited William Butler Yeats's 'The Fiddler of Dooney':

When I play on my fiddle in Dooney,
folk dance like a wave of the sea;
My cousin is priest in Kilvarnet,
My brother in Mocharabuiee.

I passed my brother and cousin:
They read in their books of prayer:
I read in my book of songs
I bought at the Sligo fair.

And I guess this made sense, because both poems were about ordinary people who were sure of themselves, sure of what they did, where they belonged, what their purpose in life was.

And I was not sure where I belonged or what my own purpose in life was back then, even though I had trained as a painter in Jamaica and New York and I was in London on a training programme as a copywriter at one of the world's largest advertising agencies. But listening to those three Irish men recite 'The Fiddler of Dooney' that afternoon, maybe I'd thought yes, that's what I'd like to be, someone whose artistry makes people dance like a wave of the sea. If I thought that, I then forgot about it. For many years I forgot about wanting to make people feel as if they were part of the cosmic dance, in tune with life's rhythm like a wave of the sea.

That day, after the Irishmen recited William Butler Yeats's words in that tea shop on Marylebone High Street, silence fell. You know how sometimes when you are in a group laughing and talking and then suddenly everyone becomes quiet and you know that the gathering has come to an end because the spirit of the meeting has declared the gathering adjourned? We all got up at the same time and walked out into the late afternoon sunshine. We five stood around awkwardly on the pavement for a while, saying things like, 'Well, alright then…' 'You take care now,' 'Really nice to have met you,' and 'Good-oh.'

There were no addresses or telephone numbers exchanged, no, 'How about we meet up for lunch (or tea or dinner)?' Helen and the alpha male gazed meaningfully at each other one last time. Then we all turned and went off in different directions.

2

A Taste of Honey

I'M ALMOST CERTAIN that I saw it at the Regal; but it was over fifty years ago, so it is possible that I did in fact see it at the State Theatre, which showed mostly 'art' films. I am almost positive that I did not see it at the Carib, where my siblings and I often sat happily through Saturday afternoon matinees. I am going to go with the Regal Theatre, where I saw many a movie and quite a few stage-shows featuring some of my favourite Jamaican singers like Toots and the Maytals, Marcia Griffiths, Judy Mowatt, Alton Ellis and Roy Shirley. Once, in that same theatre, I even saw a live reading of Dylan Thomas's 'A Boy Growing Up', by the famous Welsh actor Emlyn Williams. For the record: the city of Kingston once had over twenty active, well-supported theatres and cinemas, including three drive-in theatres.

Perhaps because I come from a very big family I'd learned from an early age to cherish any time I spent alone, and this would explain why I'd thought nothing of going by

myself to the Regal one Saturday afternoon in 1963 to see
A *Taste of Honey*.

The movie had been adapted from the play by the British
writer Shelagh Delaney. I did not know this then, but she was
eighteen years old when she wrote it, just a few years older
than I was at the time I saw it, and Shelagh Delaney never
knew this, but she changed my life.

It was many years after seeing that film that I read about
Shelagh Delaney. She was considered 'ineducable' and failed
her 11-plus four times, but through sheer determination
made it to grammar school only to leave early to find
employment in a number of dead-end jobs.

But somehow Shelagh Delaney, as I understand it, knew
that she was a writer. She had a father who was a great
storyteller and two grandparents who instilled in her a love
of language and, long story short, she went to a play one
night because she'd been introduced to drama at school by
a teacher who'd seen something in her. Shelagh Delaney
went to a play that she found boring, pretentious and
condescending, and said to herself, I can do better than that,
and went home and wrote A *Taste of Honey*, which started
as a novel, but, as she was young and wanting to be out
and about and going dancing, she took two weeks off from
whatever going-nowhere job she had at the time, and turned
the novel into a play that won her a BAFTA award. She went
on to produce plays, short stories, films and TV scripts up
until she died at the age of seventy-one.

Some years before I saw A *Taste of Honey*, I'd had
another experience similar to my epiphany in the Regal
Theatre that Saturday afternoon. This had happened in an
English literature class at school, when we read *The Family
from One End Street* by Eve Garnett who had been an art

student when she'd written and illustrated this engaging story for children. That book was one of the first set in modern times that I'd ever read in which the main characters were solidly working class. The father of the Ruggles family was a dustman and the mother took in washing and ironing, and there were seven children.

As one of nine children, I found it reassuring to know that such families lived in England, a country you would assume – if you were to judge by most of the books we'd been given to read in school up till then – was populated mostly by lords and ladies, and by chimney sweeps and serving maids who would rise with some effort to one day become lords and ladies. I would never have known then about families like the one Eve Garnett wrote about if I had not read that book – families who were lower down on the economic ladder than my own. My father worked at the telephone company, where he installed telephones; Mr Ruggles was a dustman. My mother was a gifted dressmaker while Mrs Ruggles took in washing and ironing. My parents employed a woman to do our washing and ironing. So while I did identify with Eve Garnett's book, which won the Carnegie Medal and is now regarded as a classic of children's literature, I am ashamed to admit that I felt somewhat better off than Lily Rose and her brothers and sisters, just as many of my friends in high school, who lived in really nice houses in upper St Andrew, felt they were better off than me because my family did not.

But that Saturday afternoon in the Regal Theatre (I'm going with the Regal Theatre, especially as it, like most of Kingston's movie theatres, no longer exists) I was glad that I'd gone to see *A Taste of Honey* by myself because I remember being so moved that I could not stop crying. I identified fully with the character of the teenage girl who was a gifted artist racked by self-doubt, anxious about the level of her own intelligence and about her place in life.

I was both fascinated and appalled by the mother who goes off and marries a fancy man leaving the girl to fend for herself. The girl becomes pregnant by a handsome Black sailor who goes off to sea, presumably never to be heard from again, and the girl is then befriended by a young homosexual man who tells her 'You need somebody to love you, while you are looking for someone to love.' They move in together and he begins to look after her and to prepare for the arrival of the baby. The movie ends on a heart-wrenching note as the bad mother, who has been abandoned by her new husband, comes back into her daughter's life and forces out the young man who had been tenderly making arrangements for the birth of the baby. The girl is played by one of the brightest stars of 60s British stage and screen, Rita Tushingham, who also played the daughter of Dr Zhivago and Lara in David Lean's gorgeous epic *Doctor Zhivago*.

Another reason this movie is transformative was recently revealed to me by the writer Caz Phillips. When the girl asks him where he was born, the Black sailor replies that he's from Cardiff. This is the first time that a Black character in a film ever identified themselves as British.

It took me a long time to understand why I was so moved by *A Taste of Honey*, but I finally figured out that it was probably the first film I saw where I felt sympathy for the humanity of every single one of the characters, even for the careless living mother who was the exact antithesis of my own. My heart ached for the young gay man, who demonstrates more maternal concern for the arrival of the baby than the pregnant girl does, and the scene near the end, where the awful mother hands him back the bassinet he'd bought for the baby, was one of the saddest things I'd ever seen.

There was not a lot of happiness on offer in that film; still it proved to be one of the most important experiences I would ever have in a cinema, because I decided to myself as I sat there in the dark that no matter what I was going to do with my life I would somehow try to honour the humanity of everyone, no matter how strange, how different, how not-usual. Jamaican society is notoriously homophobic, and I credit that movie with helping me to honour the humanity of gay people and of people who do not fit in.

Shelagh Delaney was pronounced 'ineducable', but was able to produce work that affected me so deeply that I ended up sitting alone in a cinema after everybody else had filed out, trying hard to compose myself enough to go outside and face a world where most people would not understand why a simple thing like a Saturday afternoon matinee could make me weep as if a close friend or relative had died.

3

Some poems that made me

FROM THE TIME I was maybe seven or eight years old, I began to be seized by a strong desire to put down my feelings in writing. Before that, I'd mostly expressed my feelings orally, sometimes in rhyme. One of my first rhyming efforts took the form of what I considered to be a praise song to my mother's distant cousin, Mimi Blackie. The rhyme had something to do with cousin Mimi's fondness for the Jamaican national fruit, the ackee:

Miss Mimi Blackie
She love to eat ackee

For this, my mother cautioned me that I was being disrespectful to one of her beloved relatives from Harvey River. After that I decided that it was best to write things down. But setting my thoughts down in writing also managed to get me into trouble, especially after I took it upon myself to write, on the newly painted walls of the family toilet, something that I had read in the obituary section of *The Gleaner*. To this day I still cannot comprehend why I was so affected by the headline: 'Mrs Hilda Shoucair is dead'. I had never met the lady, and I am certain that nobody in my family had ever had anything to do with her. Why then was I so moved by the news of her death that I felt compelled to write of it on that wall?

'Mrs Hilda Shoucair is dead'.

I got punished for that. Many years later I would learn from my husband, Ted Chamberlin, how some of the earliest poems recorded were words written on tombstones in remembrance of the dead. Wherever Mrs H. Shoucair is, I hope she knows that in keeping with this tradition, I tried to make sure that she was not forgotten and that I suffered for my art. And yet whenever I am asked, 'When did you know that you were a poet?' or 'When did you write your first poem?' I never think back to this incident, I usually say that the first poem I ever wrote was 'After A Shower of Rain'. I wrote it in the aftermath of one of those sudden downpours that come to quench the Jamaican landscape in the month of August. It is the kind of rain that cleans the air and the trees and which leaves behind the most pleasing of all scents, 'eau de rain on dry earth'. This kind of shower is usually followed by swarms of 'rainflies' who dance around electric lights until you hold a bowl of water up close to the light bulb so they can dive to their death by drowning.

I was not the kind of child who saved my school books, so I'll never be able to revisit my earliest poetic efforts, but looking back now I realise that apart from early babbling and doodling (like my couplets for Mimi Blackie and Mrs H. Shoucair) maybe I first came to poetry through the hymns that I sang at my Convent infant school, where I learned to sing praises to the Virgin Mary, and All Saints Primary School, and St Hugh's High School for Girls where every school day started with the singing of a good Anglican hymn. Poetry also presented itself early in the nursery rhymes, riddles, songs and poems my mother would sing or recite to us, like the numinous, riddling 'Who Has Seen the Wind?' by Christina Rossetti.

Who has seen the wind?
Neither you nor I:
But when the trees bow down their heads,
the wind is passing by.

Poetry wafted in off the streets in the cries of the mango sellers who would go about the city of Kingston calling out:

Call: Buy yu number eleven
Response: Mango
Call: Buy yu Hairy, hairy
Response: Mango
Call: Buy yu Blackie
Response: Mango
Call: Buy yu sweetie-come brush me
Response: Mango

Poetry provided the imagery for the ring games I played as a small girl:

'There's a brown girl in the ring, tra la la la la' (Boney M later turned this traditional Jamaican children's song into a big hit). And it provided the rhythm when we jumped rope:

Massquitta one, massquitta two
Massquitta jump inna hot callaloo.

My mother had been a teacher of small children before she married my father and had nine children of her own and she would tell me and my siblings stories at night before we went to sleep. The story of the little Hebrew boy Samuel who was the only one that Yahweh cared to address his precious words to at a time when Yahweh was withholding his speech from his chosen people, was one of our family favourites. She would accompany the story by singing the hymn:

Hushed was the evening hymn,
The temple courts were dark,
The lamp was burning dim,
Before the sacred ark:
When suddenly a voice divine
Rang through the silence of the shrine.

Oh, give me Samuel's ear,
The open ear, O Lord,
Alive and quick to hear
Each whisper of Thy word!

Like all children, I thought literally, so I was deeply puzzled at first by the idea of asking to be given someone's ear. Wouldn't that mean that I would have three ears and the poor little boy just one? Also, 'Alive and quick'? 'Alive' yes, but what was a 'quick ear'? Still, I liked the sound of these words, and soon I just decided to go along with that and not worry too much about the business of the ears. If I imagined that Samuel was a little boy who lived at All Saints Church, where my family then worshipped, I could quite clearly see the picture that was being painted.

I count this as one of the poems that made me, because I am always hoping to be given the open ear that is alive and quick to hear each whisper of the word, the good word, the singing mysterious word that is Poetry.

Another poem that helped to shape me was William Wordsworth's 'I Wandered Lonely as a Cloud', aka 'The Daffodils'. Over the years I have said quite a lot about this poem, as have other writers throughout the British Commonwealth who have come to regard it as the ultimate anthem to British colonial oppression.

What I will say here is that that poem caused me to wonder why, as a Jamaican child of eight or nine, I was being made to memorise and recite a poem about a flower I had never seen, a flower that does not grow on the island. And perhaps because as a small child I had asked for an open ear, I thought I heard a voice saying, 'Well maybe you should write a poem about the plants and flowers that grow in Jamaica,' and I have tried to obey that voice.

The next poem that helped to shape my poetic voice was Leigh Hunt's 'Abou Ben Adhem'. This was another poem I'd been made to memorise at primary school by our headmaster Ralston Wilmot, who was a gentleman, a humanist, and a great lover of literature and music.

I was told a few years ago by someone who is a speaker of Arabic that the title of this poem is problematic – 'Abou' means 'son of' and 'Ben' also means 'son of' – but this has not changed my feelings towards it. I liked 'Abou Ben Adhem' so much that I took to reciting it sometimes when I accompanied my mother to weddings where she had designed and sewn the bride's and bridesmaids' dresses. As a kind of two-for-one deal, the assembled guests would be able to admire my mother's peerless dressmaking even as they were treated to my rendition of 'Abou Ben Adhem'. I guess these recitations can be counted as my first poetry readings.

And then there is Rupert Brooke's poem about the little dog who went on a tear and, of course, paid for it with his life. I learned that poem at St Hugh's High School for Girls, set up in Kingston, Jamaica over 115 years ago by the Church of England. Our patron saint was St Hugh of Lincoln, we wore two-piece shirt-waist uniforms of Lincoln green and under our pleated skirts we were required to wear knee-length bloomers. No other footwear was permitted except dark brown lace-up Oxfords, and dark brown socks, and on our heads we wore green berets. Because our patron saint was alleged to have had a pet swan who always followed him around, our school badge was a small cobalt-blue enamelled shield, upon which a swan floated on the waves of the word *Fidelitas*. The schoolboys of Kingston called us 'green lizards'. We referred to ourselves as swans.

At age twelve, I sat in a classroom with a high ceiling and listened as our English teacher, who was from England, read us, with no warning or preparation, two poems: T.S. Eliot's 'The Journey of the Magi' and Rupert Brooke's 'The Little Dog's Day'. The look of pure delight on her face as she read them aloud was enough to show us how poems can give pleasure. That same teacher, her name was Mrs Junor, also read us sections of 'The Love Song of J. Alfred Prufrock', and I remember being completely captivated by her performance. But she did not explain those poems, and she never gave us one piece of biographical information about the poets; we were allowed to let the words do whatever they wished to us, and I believe they worked some kind of magic on my twelve-year-old self. I cannot, to this day, read those poems without being overtaken by a great sense of delight, although in actual fact the subject of 'The

Love Song of J. Alfred Prufrock' is really deeply depressing. But I thoroughly enjoyed them, and I am still charmed by 'The Little Dog's Day' by Rupert Brooke, particularly by the opening stanza, with its gentle description of people asleep and the sun rising; a deceptive start to what would prove to be a day of riotous canine infamy. I liked it that the dog began his twenty-four-hour spree of doggy wickedness with a dance; and maybe because of this I have always liked the idea of writing about dancing in poems.

Nine years later, when I was a student at the Art Students League of New York I bought, from Brentano's bookstore in Greenwich Village, a copy of Rupert Brooke's poems and I read them as I rode the subway. I particularly liked the poems from the section on the South Seas; one I kept revisiting was 'The Great Lover':

> *I have been so great a lover: filled my days*
> *So proudly with the splendour of Love's praise,*
> *The pain, the calm, and the astonishment,*
> *Desire illimitable, and still content,*
> *And all dear names men* [and women] *use, to cheat*
> *   despair.*

In a beautiful and strange come around, a few years ago I was given a copy of that same collection by George Kiddell, a wonderful Canadian who played a big part in acquiring my papers for the Fisher Library at the University of Toronto. My husband, Ted, and I spent several evenings in his company at his apartment in Toronto, and towards the end of those evenings the three of us would inevitably end up reciting poems aloud. George Cadell also liked Rupert Brooke, and just before he died he sent me a leather-bound early edition of *1914 & Other Poems* as a gift to replace my dog-eared copy, which I had long since left behind on the seat of a New York subway.

Looking back, I see that I was taught a very wide range of poems, almost all written by European men. Poems like Alfred Noyes's 'The Highwayman', Tennyson's 'The Lady of Shalott', Rudyard Kipling's 'If' and many of Shakespeare's sonnets. I learned to take delight in poems like Walter de la Mare's 'The Listeners' and the mad funny verses of Ogden Nash and Hilaire Belloc. To this day if I find myself in the company of old school friends like Cecile Clayton and Annie Rose Kitchin, we are liable to end up reciting the long cautionary tale in verse of Belloc's 'Jim', who was eaten by a lion for the crime of running away from his nursemaid.

I was also taught several of the poems of John Masefield – who used local language – and these are so hard-wired into me that occasionally, for no apparent reason, I will find myself crooning 'The Port of Many Ships'.

It's a sunny pleasant anchorage, is Kingdom Come,
Where crews is always layin' aft with double-tots o' rum,
'N' there's dancin' 'n' fiddlin' of ev'ry kind o' sort,
It's a fine place for sailormen is that there port
'N' I wish—
I wish as I was there.

The winds is never nothin' more than jest light airs,
'N' no one gets belayin' pinned, 'n' no one never swears.

To be fair to our teacher, in this case she did explain to us that to be 'belayin' pinned' is essentially to get whacked over the head with a heavy blunt instrument shaped like a rolling pin.

Some poems that made me

When my father died in December 1963, I felt as if I had been belayin' pinned. Like all my siblings I had to struggle to make sense of this terrible loss and of the dramatic changes that my father's death brought about in our family. One of these changes was that I was sent to live with my elder sister Barbara and her husband, Ancile Gloudon, in their beautiful home in Gordon Town in the foothills of the Blue Mountains. My sister, who is one of the brightest and best-known women in the Caribbean and who has had an outstanding career as a journalist and radio talk show host, has always been a great reader, and the library in that house was well stocked with a wide range of books, including a signed first edition copy of *The Dream Keeper and Other Poems* by Langston Hughes. I was overjoyed to discover these poems by this revered and iconic figure of African American poetry, and I got no end of pleasure from reading lyrics like 'Weary Blues', 'Dream Variations' and 'Quiet Girl'.

On the shelves that ran floor to ceiling in that long narrow library, there were many signed first editions of books written by early authors of West Indian literature, several of whom were personal friends of my sister and her husband. Outstanding books from the *New York Times* bestseller list had also made it on to the shelves as well as a complete set of textbooks acquired from a close friend of my brother-in-law's who had read English at the University of the West Indies.

In between studying the texts I was meant to be doing for my O-level English exams, I read widely from that library, sometimes drawn by the illustrations on the book jackets. For example, I was attracted to Giuseppe di Lampedusa's great family saga *The Leopard* because the book jacket featured a rampant leopard on a coat of arms, set against a scarlet background. But Vic Reid's novel *The Leopard* actually resonated more with me because he is such an important Jamaican writer whom I was lucky enough to meet in person on a few occasions. James Baldwin's *Another Country*, Richard Wright's *Native Son* and Ralph Ellison's *Invisible Man* were all important works of fiction I first encountered there; but I always returned to the lower shelves where the collections of poetry were kept. I developed a fondness for one particular collection featuring the metaphysical poets John Donne and George Herbert. I found John Donne hard going, and most of the time I just could not puzzle out his extravagant conceits, but I am certain that I benefited from the trying. George Herbert was way more accessible, and that is because I was used to singing some of his poems that had been set to hymn tunes in church and at school. At least once a month, we'd sing 'The Elixir' in school assembly, and when we did I'd always find myself puzzling over these two stanzas:

A man that looks on glass,
On it may stay his eye;
Or if he pleaseth, through it pass,
And then the heav'n espy.

This is the famous stone
That turneth all to gold;
For that which God doth touch and own
cannot for less be told.

George Herbert's lyrics seemed always to be concerned with some mysterious and healing source of goodness that I really wanted to get close to, but I had no idea how I'd be able to do this except through reading poems like his. Roaming freely through those bookshelves was the beginning of my lifelong identification with the figure of the scholar gypsy in Matthew Arnold's long poem 'Thyrsis', and I am still, to this day, drawn to poems that contain what I call 'medicine' in them.

But when I found *In a Green Night*, an early collection of poems by Derek Walcott, who had been at university with my brother-in-law, was a good friend of my sister's, and became a mentor and good friend to me, I stopped reading everything else and took to just reading his poems.

I read *In a Green Night* in the way I sometimes read the Hebrew Psalms (King James version), seeking something to hold on to: poem as source of hope and consolation; poem as lifeboat, anchor and safe harbour.

One of the many things I liked about Walcott's poems was that they alluded to people and landscapes with which I was familiar, and I badly needed to be on safe familiar ground right then as my father, the North Star of our family, the light of our lives, was gone.

One poem in particular, 'A Careful Passion', became one I kept returning to, not just because of the subject of the poem – doomed angst-ridden love (as a teenager I was of course deeply taken with anything that was angst-ridden) but because a number of things about it taught me how a poem could be written in a fresh and engaging way.

First, the epigraph in Jamaican vernacular made me see that patois could be used for something other than humour, and that in fact no other epigraph would have been as appropriate:

Hosanna I build me house, Lawd,
De rain come wash it 'way.

Then the opening lines employed language that could have been found in an advertisement for high-end real estate or in a tourism brochure:

The Cruise Inn, at the city's edge,
Extends a breezy prospect of the sea...

It then went on to incorporate brilliant metaphors:

From tables fixed like islands near a hedge
Of foam-white flowers...

In that poem, an old Greek freighter is quitting port, no doubt making way for a Caribbean schooner helmed by Walcott. It is not his greatest poem, but it is still one of my favourites by him, because it has so many fine turns.

So cha cha cha, begin the long goodbyes...

The cha cha is a dance where one steps forwards and backwards and marks time on the spot; who has not said such a goodbye? Also, 'cha cha cha', if pronounced by someone with a Jamaican accent, can sound like 'chu chu chu', a cry of deep frustration sounded three times.

I liked that you could do that in a poem, but back then it never occurred to me that I would ever produce a book of poetry, nor that at some point I'd become deeply invested in trying for the kinds of skilful turns I have always instinctively admired in great writing. I suppose I was always, from the very beginning, just feeling my way forward.

About a year after I started reading *In a Green Night* I was given a prize for English Literature at St Hugh's. It was *The Oxford Book of Modern Verse* edited by W. B. Yeats. I have read this anthology from cover to cover many times. One of the first things I did was to search through it for the works of women writers. I have to confess that only a few of them stayed with me – some pieces by Lady Gregory, from the Irish of Douglas Hyde. But there was a poet named Michael Field – I did not know then that it was the pen name of two women – who wrote some pretty angst-ridden verse that caused me to weep copious and cleansing tears.

Anyway, I got way more pleasure from reading poets like Oliver St John Gogarty, Ernest Dowson, Rabindranath Tagore, and Yeats himself, and I kept returning to one particular poem by Walter James Turner. I later found out he was a theatre critic. Turner's 'Hymn To Her Unknown' was a revelation to me, and it taught me a great deal about the writing of poetry. It starts off as reportage, who, what, where, when, and then gradually becomes more and more freighted with rhythm, rhyme, repetition, allusion, rendering the language more and more patterned, more dense until the voice in the poem is almost talking in tongues before Venus rising from the waves is referenced, thus cooling things off. I taught that poem at the University of Michigan for many years and I recommend it highly.

But all these poems were written by men; and as I began to think more and more about my own place in the world I really, really needed to hear and read poems written by people who looked and thought like me. I searched through *The Oxford Book of Modern Verse* looking for poems to which I, as a Black woman, could relate, until I came across three poems that had Africa as their subject. One by Edith Sitwell – whose bold confident writing style was of some interest until I came to her truly appalling poem 'Gold Coast Customs'. Dread! There was also one by Roy Campbell, titled 'The Zulu Girl' and one called 'The Scorpion' by William Plomer.

The unsettling way in which all these poets quickly turned to animal analogies to describe Black people made me feel queasy, Sitwell's poem being the absolute worst and Roy Campbell's being the least worst. After that experience I knew that I needed to find poems that did not disrespect people like me, poems that honoured the humanity of my people.

Maybe if I had known more about Elizabeth Barrett Browning when I was searching for women poets to read I'd have spent more time with her work back then – I'd been made to memorise 'How Do I Love Thee?' – because her family had strong ties to Jamaica. The Barretts have deep roots in my homeland, as they used to own several large sugar estates where they profited handsomely from the unpaid labour of enslaved Africans. It was years later that I read how the source of her family's income was apparently deeply troubling to Elizabeth Barrett Browning, who once wrote, 'I belong to a family of West Indian slaveholders, and if I believed in curses, I should be afraid.' The concern for freedom and justice which drove many of her works stemmed from the fact that she felt guilty about profiting from the proceeds of such monumental cruelty and injustice.

The late 1960s and early 1970s were all about freedom and justice for me; it was also the time when I really began to accept the fact that I am a poet, and when I began to actively search out the works of Black women poets who might become role models for me. When I studied painting at the Art Students League of New York, I spent a good deal of time reading the fearless and incendiary writings of African American women poets like Sonia Sanchez, Nikki Giovanni, June Jordan, Lucille Clifton and others, and I even tried for some of their righteously wrathful turns in a few of my early efforts, but I eventually came to the conclusion that, much as I love and admire these poets, I had to keep searching for my own unique way of expressing myself, which can accurately represent my own life experiences and my own culture.

In retrospect, I'd say that the African American woman poet whose work nourished me the most was Gwendolyn Brooks; her voice is truly elegant and timeless. And the great fiction writers like Zora Neale Hurston, Toni Cade Bambara, Paule Marshall and Toni Morrison are all writers whose work I greatly respect and admire.

But all this time I kept searching for poetry written by Caribbean women, only coming across the odd poem here and there because they were hard to locate in print back then. I'd heard of Una Marson from my parents because she came from the same part of the island as my father – the parish of St Elizabeth – and occasionally I'd come across one of her poems in the local newspaper, my personal favourite being 'Kinky Hair Blues', but I was not taught the work of any Jamaican women writers at school. I was vaguely familiar with the names of a few other women writers like Barbara Ferland, Constance Hollar and Vera Bell, who wrote one really powerful poem called 'Ancestor on the Auction Block', but at that time none of these women occupied a really central place in Caribbean literature. As proof of this, in 1971 when Bolivar Press in Kingston published a slim and handsome volume titled *Seven Jamaican Poets*, that publication did not include one work by a woman, although by then the great Louise Bennett had been writing and performing her poems for decades.

That the poems of Louise Bennett eventually managed to find their way into *The Norton Anthology of Modern and Contemporary Poetry* was largely due to the efforts of the brilliant literary critic Jahan Ramazani, and was a case of justice being served, because, while I grew up familiar with Louise Bennett's extraordinary satirical poems, Jamaicans were not encouraged to regard what she did as real poetry because she wrote in Jamaican English. All modern Jamaican and Caribbean writers owe Miss Lou a great debt because she took a great deal of abuse from the gatekeepers of society so that Jamaicans could one day be proud of the way we speak and write.

As far as poetry written by women was concerned, the 1960s and 70s were all about Sylvia Plath, and I learned one of the most important lessons of my life, my writing life, from reading Plath's work. I learned that there are writers whose words are so powerful, whose ideas and images are so seductive, that a young writer can lose their own way by trying to follow them.

Sylvia Plath has written some of the most compelling poems in the English language. 'Lady Lazarus', with its multiple deaths and resurrections and reinventions, is the one I value most as I look back at my own, now long life, but I sensed early on that it was dangerous for me to spend too much time in Plath's company because her world view is so inclined to be dark, and because for much of my young life I was so wounded, wayward and impressionable. I mercifully sensed that for my soul's safety I needed to hold on to things that are life-affirming.

This need to hold on to what is life-giving also influenced my readings of Anne Sexton, and to some extent Virginia Woolf. I decided along the way to always approach the work of some writers with a measure of caution and respect, and to remind myself always that my admiration for their work did not mean that they would be ideal role models for me.

Some poems that made me

Edna St Vincent Millay was the exception to my rule. Some of the earliest poems by women I had found had been written by her, and I immediately took to her voice because I liked that she professed to being a sort of wild woman, and at the time I was getting ready to try on that persona for myself. Her influence on me was made manifest in the form of a longish mawkish rhyming poem I wrote which was heavily patterned on her long poem 'Renascence'. Even at seventeen I realised how bad my effort was, so I tore it up. But looking back now, I'm sure that the writing of it helped me to process my grief at the loss of my father because it was a poem about resurrection, renewal and coming back to life.

I would say that the poem that has had the greatest impact on my adult life is the *Divine Comedy*. My engagement with it began when I was one of several poets invited by the Southbank Centre in London to rewrite one of the Cantos from Dante's masterpiece. To date I have rewritten seven cantos, setting them all in Jamaica and employing Jamaican dialect in tribute to the great Italian poet who wrote in the local language of his people.

So, I really ended up writing the poems that I wanted to read, and writing them in a way that sounds more like the language I use when I quarrel with myself, or when I lament, praise, pray and console myself and hopefully others. A friend of mine once said that the poetry I have written can be grouped into two categories: poems about love, and poems about justice. That is probably true, and of this I am certain: I intend to keep praying for the open ear, in order to hear them if and when they come.

4

Nadine Gordimer Memorial Lecture

'Guinea Woman'

My great grandmother was a Guinea woman.
Wide eyes turning the corners of her face
could see behind her.
Her cheeks dusted with a fine rash of jet-bead warts
that itched when the rain set up.
Great grandmother's waistline the span of a
headman's
hand. Slender and tall like a cane stalk
with a Guinea woman's antelope-quick walk.
And when she paused, her gaze would look to see
her profile fine like some obverse impression
on a Guinea coin from Royal memory.
It seems her fate was anchored in that unfathomable
sea,
for great grandmother caught the eye of a sailor
whose ship sailed without him from Lucea Harbour.

Great grandmother's royal scent of cinnamon and
    scallions
drew the sailor up the straits of Africa; the evidence
is my blue-eyed grandmother, the first mulatta
taken into backra's household and covered with his
    name.
They forbade great grandmother's Guinea woman
    presence,
they washed away her scent of cinnamon and scallions.
They controlled the child's antelope walk, and they called
    her uprisings, rebellions.
But great grandmother, I see your features, blood dark
    appearing
in the children of each new breeding. And the high
    yellow-brown
is darkening down: Listen children, it's your great
    grandmother's turn.

IT MAY HAVE begun some time in 1965, with hearing Miriam Makeba and Harry Belafonte singing 'The Train Song'. Or it could have begun with hearing Hugh Masekela's rendition of 'Coal Train', and then finding out what the words meant. How these trains were taking migrant workers away from their homes and families in Southern Africa to those wicked and dreadful minefields, to excavate the great wealth from which they themselves could not profit, their humanity regarded then as less-than.

And something in you felt you had to keep track of that train and always follow the fortunes of those men and their women and children.

It may even have begun as far back as 1959 when you heard your parents saying how proud they were that our then premier Norman Manley had made Jamaica one of the first countries to join the embargo against trading with South Africa. You are not sure exactly when.

But one day you became convinced that your people, including your writers and scholars, artists and singers and players of instruments, had a burden placed upon them to speak and write and sing without cease of the fate of our Southern African brethren and sistren – yea, until Apartheid's end.

Her name was Daphne Abrahams; and she was white; she was one of my first art teachers and she was the first South African I'd ever seen in real life. But most evenings I'd hear her husband's voice over the radio. His name was Peter and he was Black and he was dearly loved and respected by the people of Jamaica. Peter and Daphne Abrahams were guilty of a love deemed criminal under Apartheid, but they found a place to thrive in Jamaica where they lived up in the hills and he wrote his great novels following *Mine Boy* and talked to us through the radio about things particular and universal, local and foreign, spiritual and secular, and always ended his broadcasts with life-giving words of encouragement.

And please know that the people of Jamaica truly loved Peter Abrahams and that we too are heartbroken and mortified by how his life ended. Peter Abrahams was the first writer from South Africa I really knew, but I'd read about the consequences of a marriage like his and Daphne's in the novels of Alan Paton, in *Cry, the Beloved Country* and *Too Late the Phalarope*.

Then in the summer of 1968 on my first trip to the USA, I caught Hugh Masekela at the Village Gate, 'Grazing in the Grass'. The manager was Jamaican, and he allowed me and my two friends, Lorna Bennett and Joy Rogers, to stay over and watch the second show for free because we were so obviously young-girl delighted by Mr Masekela himself in his striped bell-bottom pants, and by his trumpet stylings, his exquisite artistry: exuberance and joy as fellow travellers accompanying profound sorrow songs of unfreedom.

That condition of being at home with great contradiction – joy and sorrow, humour in the midst of grim realities, and stubborn, sometimes slenderest of hope in the midst of massive despair – is one of the great gifts that the artists, writers and thinkers of the continent of Africa and of the African diaspora have given to the world.

Something else they have given the world is a way of being entirely at home with the unempirical gifts of prophecy. That Nelson Mandela would say time and again, 'South Africa Will Be Free – pause – In My Lifetime' was always a source of wonder to many, myself included. How could he have said these words repeatedly, given what he was up against?

But he spoke them, and he wrote them, and he said them again and again, and Alleluia they came to pass, and everyone who trades in words should meditate a while upon that. Now more than ever we must believe that, as Rastafarians say, 'word sounds have power'.

In 1983 I had the great good fortune to take part in the Iowa International Writing Program at the University of Iowa, where writers from all over the world are brought together for a semester and given time and resources to write, give readings and lectures, and to be part of a community of writers and scholars learning from one another. I shared living space in the big adult dormitory of the Mayflower Hotel with a writer from South Africa by the name of Gladys Thomas. Here is my poem for her:

Redemption Ground

'The Woman in Gladys's Story'

Struck a match and smelled sulphur scorch the yellow
wallpaper rose. Like Dido she torches her own bed.
Introduced as my South African flatmate we are
meant to share a kitchen. I see her light skin,
she reads my face and says 'I'm coloured'.

Her story is set in district six, Cape Town where she
and her husband Albert made life, making art. Black
and White Indian Chinese and Coloured mixed
till the state roared in with tear gas
and attack dogs.

Gladys shows snapshots of her husband then doing
*   ninety days*
for staging Bertolt Brecht's Mother Courage. *He is*
*   standing*
outside their good brick house; around his feet
a riot of yellow flowers. Uprooted
into hardscrabble township.

She considered setting fire to the house; but chose instead
to hand the woman in her story kerosene and matches.
We cook a chicken dinner; break the wishbone:
Free South Africa! Talk till we can see through
the windows of the Mayflower

the Chinese writer executing a kata along the Iowa's
*   jade green*
banks. He spends waking hours outdoors after being ten
years locked down in a cell because of a story he wrote.
In our shared kitchen we brew strong black tea
We applaud his morning dance.

Nadine Gordimer Memorial Lecture

When I said goodbye to Gladys in 1983, we never thought that we would see each other again. Ours was one tearful parting. Unlike Nelson Mandela – the Prophet, Warrior-king, Peacemaker, Repairer of the Breach, Father of the Nation and new-human-being-cultured-over-twenty-seven-years-for-the-benefit-of-all-humanity – I was not at all sure that South Africa would be free in this lifetime.

And all someone like me could do was to participate in countless anti-Apartheid rallies and grieve about the conditions under which someone like Winnie Mandela lived and suffered as a banned person.

And one day I was walking along the street in the city of Kingston and a clipping from a newspaper, right there on the sidewalk, caught my eye. The news story stated that Winnie Mandela's home had been raided by the police, and that they had seized a number of her personal items in this raid, including a bedspread. The bedspread had been taken into custody because it was in the colours of the flag of the African National Congress. That had to be a poem.

'Bedspread'

Sometimes in the still unchanging afternoons
when the memories crowded hot and hopeless
against her brow, she would seek its cool colours
and signal him to lie down in his cell.
It is three in the afternoon, Nelson.
Let us lie here together on this bright bank draped
in Freedom colour.
It was woven by women with slender capable hands
accustomed to binding wounds.
Hands that closed the eyes of dead children

that fought for the right to speak in their own lands
in their own schools.

They wove the bedspread and knotted notes of hope
in each strand, and selvaged the edges with ancient
  blessings
older than any white man's coming.
Nelson my husband I meet you in dreams.
Beloved, much of the world too is asleep.
Blind to the tyranny and evil devouring our people.
But Mandela you are rock on this sand.
harder than any metal in the bowels of this land
You are purer than any gold tempered by fire.
Shall we lie here wrapped in the colours of our free
  Azania?

They arrested the bedspread. They and their friends
  are working
to arrest the dreams in our heads.
But the women accustomed to closing the eyes of the
  dead
are weaving cloths still brighter, to drape us in glory
in a free Azania.

I had the honour of reading that poem to Winnie when the Mandelas visited Jamaica right after his release from prison.

For many of us writers and artists and musicians in the African diaspora, Africa is never far from our minds. And South Africa never, ever left our minds during the time of Apartheid.

Under the British colonial school system in Jamaica, we were never taught that there was such a thing as an African writer; but for me the living presence of Peter Abrahams in Jamaica was proof that Africans did write books, and this led to my discovery of other African writers like Chinua Achebe, Ngugi Wa Thiong'o and Wole Soyinka. But the women – I needed to find the women writers of Africa. The women who were the scribes who had set down those stories that used to be scripted by tongues and stored in books of memory. Women writers who would look and sound more like me, whose stories would perhaps help to connect me to a place and a time and a history and to traditions lost in the great watery graveyard of the Atlantic.

So I went in search of the work of African women writers, and as time went on I actually had the privilege of meeting and even on occasion sharing a stage with some of them, including the venerable Ama Ata Aidoo, Tsitsi Dangarembga and our own dear Miriam Tlali, who once told me that during the time of Apartheid she would sometimes write her stories then wrap them in plastic bags and bury them in her backyard in case her home was raided by the police. Miriam Tlali, Bessie Head, Olive Schreiner, Doris Lessing, Noni Jabavu, Phyllis Ntantala-Jordan and Ingrid Jonker are no longer with us, but we owe them a great debt for the ways in which their lives and works have nourished and sustained humanity.

And then of course there is the great iconic figure: Nadine Gordimer.

I had the enormous privilege of meeting Mrs Gordimer – I always call her Mrs Gordimer – at a Commonwealth writers conference in Manchester, England, organised by the brilliant Michael Schmidt of Carcanet Press. I confess that I was star-struck. Completely starstruck. For one thing, I expected her to be much bigger in stature. And I concluded that this was because her stories are written on such a monumental scale, written with a kind of courage and power that is not usual. In real life, she was a petite and quite pretty lady who wore the most gorgeous diamond earrings I have ever seen, and who was quite comfortable wearing my husband's leather jacket one day when it rained. I believe she grew fond of Ted after she found out that he was a Professor of Comparative Literature and an expert witness in Aboriginal land claims issues and that he was instrumental in putting together a land claim for a group of Bushmen or San people in the Kalahari Desert. He wrote about all this in *If This Is Your Land, Where Are Your Stories?*

When he told Mrs Gordimer that three of the people involved in the land claim were the sisters Una, Kais and Abakas, she was visibly moved as she explained how, in 1936, she had been taken to the Empire Exhibition in Johannesburg where she saw, on display, a family of Bushmen of the Kalahari with three young girls around her age. Those girls were the same Una, Kais and Abakas whose singing, storytelling and personal witness played a big part in the success of the land claim.

And Nadine Gordimer never forgot them. It is safe to say that something transcendent must have passed between those small girls – one very privileged, staring at the three others set there in a dehumanising, objectifying display as the last of the Bushmen – a look passed between them that said, 'We see you. I see you. We see you. I see you for who you really are.'

Because something of that clear seeing shines through all of Mrs Gordimer's work; that unflinching refusal to look away from the toughest things, a determination to name them, describe them, shame them if necessary, and to fashion bold new forms to contain them as you go along. Cutting your cloth to fit your coat, as my dressmaker mother would say, in the shape of our ever-evolving, not-usual, who-knows-how-it-will-all-end story.

I want to reference here the ending to Nadine Gordimer's *July's People*. Cinematic, apocalyptic, prophetic – these days I keep reading and re-reading that ending. These days I also find myself reading and re-reading her novel *The Pickup*. I read too, her short stories that defy categorising. She is a writer that other writers learn from.

And I learned quite a few things about what women writers can bring to the writing enterprise from watching Mrs Gordimer for those few days in Manchester. For one, she had no problems with being placed on a programme with other writers who were nowhere near as accomplished and acclaimed as she was. She had the same fifteen minutes as the other three writers, the line-up went in alphabetical order, so she read second, and she had cut and pasted and timed her presentation so that it ran to exactly fifteen minutes, not a millisecond over. Done and dusted. During the question and answer period she was agreeable and amiable enough, but she also made it clear that she did not consider herself to be an acknowledged or unacknowledged legislator of the world, that she saw herself first and foremost as a writer, and that she would rather talk about matters that pertained to writing.

Coming from a writer who had been as actively politically engaged as Nadine Gordimer that was a stunning thing to hear; but it was also a freeing thing to hear for those of us who sometimes feel that there are occasions when we can best represent ourselves in the world by writing our poems and stories in such a way that they function like the look that passed between Nadine and Una, Kais and Abakas.

A look that says: I see you and I see that these are not the last days for your or for my people. In fact, we are part of a brave new future in a country that will be a shining example to the rest of the world. I see you, we see you, and we will work and suffer and struggle and rejoice together as we write this future into being.

This poem is an elegy for my mother, Doris, and I dedicate it to all the African women writers who shape and inspire us.

'After the Green Gown of My Mother Gone Down'

August, her large heart slows down then stops.
Fall now, and trees flame, catch a fire and riot

last leaves in scarlet and gold fever burning.
Remember when you heard Bob Marley hymn

'Redemption Song,' and from his tone and timbre
you sensed him traveling? He had sent the band home

and was just keeping himself company, cooling star,
sad rudeboy fretting on cowboy box guitar

in a studio with stray echo and wailing sound
lost singing scatting through the door of no return.
When the green goes, beloved, the secret is opened.
The breath falls still, the life covenant is broken.

Dress my mother's cold body in a deep green gown.
Catch a fire and let fall and flame time come,
after the green gown of my mother gone down.
We laid her down, full of days,
chant griot from the book of life,

summon her kin from the long-
lived line of David and Margaret.
Come Cleodine, Albertha,
Flavius, Edmund, Howard and Rose,
Marcus her husband gone before
come and walk Dear Doris home.

And the Blue Mountains will open to her
to seal her corporeal self in.
From the ancient vault that is their lapis lazuli heart
the headwaters of all our rivers spring.
Headwaters, wash away the embalmer's myrrh resin,
the dredging of white powder caking her cold limbs.

Return her ripe body clean
to fallow the earth.
Her eyes to become brown agate stones.
From her forehead let there dawn
bright mornings.
May her white hair contribute to the massing of
     clouds,
cause the blood settled in her palms
to sink into fish-filled lagoons.
Earth, she was a mother like you
who birthed and nursed her children.
Look, cherubim and angels, see her name
written down in the index of the faithful
in the mother-of-pearl book of saints.

Mama, Aunt Ann says
that she saw Aunt Rose
come out of an orchard
red with ripe fruit

and called out laughing to you.
And that you scaled the wall
like two young girls
scampering barefoot among
the lush fruit groves.

'My Mother's Sea Chanty'
I dream that I am washing
my mother's body in the night sea
and that she sings slow
and that she still breathes.

I see my sweet mother
a plump mermaid in my dreams
and I wash her white hair
with ambergris and foaming seaweed.

I watch my mother under water
gather the loose pearls she finds,
scrub them free from nacre
and string them on a lost fishing line.

I hear my dark mother
speaking sea-speak with pilot fish,
showing them how to direct barks
that bear away our grief.

I pray my mother breaks free
from the fish pots and marine chores
of her residence beneath the sea,
and that she rides a wild white horse.

5

I-Land

As a small child, I did not really have a very strong sense of being on an island. Maybe that is because I was born in the city of Kingston, which back then was a busy bustling metropolis, where something exciting was always happening. Kingston was no sleepy island outpost when I was growing up there. Every important person in the world seemed to pass through 'Town' as we called it, from Paul Robeson to Winston Churchill, the Bolshoi Ballet, Marion Anderson, George Bernard Shaw, Zora Neale Hurston, Sammy Davis Jr, Duke Ellington and every single member of the royal family. It was only after I began to visit my mother's birthplace, where I would bathe in the river named for her family and roam freely through the bush enjoying the pastoral delights of rural Jamaica with my cousins, that I began to think of myself as being more than a Kingstonian.

As for always looking longingly at the horizon and wondering what was beyond it – as people who live on islands are thought to do – I did not do much of that when I was a child. If I wondered what was over the horizon, it was only because my mother's sisters had emigrated to Montreal, Canada in the 1930s and they would send us letters and parcels that came from a faraway place referred to as 'abroad'.

If I had a sense of being on an island at all, it was from the way in which the people around me always described Jamaica as 'the Island of Jamaica', or 'Our Island Home'. Also, all the songs I heard or sang about Jamaica had 'island' in them. Perhaps my most vivid idea of what it was to live on an island came from my mother, who showed me that on the map of the world, Jamaica is shaped like a swimming turtle, so I got the point about being surrounded by water.

The boundary around my known world was more the boundaries set by humans, particularly by my family. I'm one of nine children. I grew up surrounded by a sea of people.

But I always loved the sensuousness of island life. I love 'sun-hot', as Jamaicans say. I enjoy bathing in the Caribbean Sea and I am certain that there are no fruits in the world that taste as good as Jamaican naseberries, mangoes, pineapples, star apples and sweetsops. Seriously nothing in the world tastes as good as a plate of Jamaican fruit. I believe that Jamaica is one of the most beautiful places in the world and I have been known to burst into tears at the sight of the Blue Mountains. In my best dreams I'm bathing in the warm Caribbean as I gaze up at the Blue Mountains. My engagement with the sheer beauty and the chaos of the island never goes away, and it drives a great deal of my work. The colours, the music, the speech, the smells, the intensity of everything, good and bad. There is nothing watered down in Jamaica, it is all concentrated and I try to draw on that.

But one of the downsides to island life is that it can be very limiting: circumscribed, provincial, petty, tribal.

Life in larger land masses such as the USA, Canada and Europe allows for much greater variety, complexity and freedom of movement. Living away from island society also allows you to change and grow and reinvent yourself away from the prying and often judgmental eyes of people who presume that because they have known you for much of your life, they are qualified to assess just what you are capable of, and to decide just how far you should go.

One of the many things I love and admire about the USA and Canada is the sense of possibility that abounds in such big places. This sense of possibility is not as available to people in island societies, and many people who experience difficulty finding ways to thrive in small island communities often grow and flourish remarkably well upon finding themselves in large metropolitan centres.

Still, I carry my islandness with me wherever I go. I always miss the sea when I'm away from it and I like to know that it is close by even if I cannot actually see it. I will even settle for a small man-made body of water – a sort of sea surrogate – like the one set down in the marshlands behind the apartment complex called The Ponds in Ann Arbor, where I lived for years. These days I am lucky to find myself living beside the Salish Sea in Halfmoon Bay, British Columbia, for being by the sea makes me feel more whole, more balanced somehow. I'd like to think it might be 'deep calleth unto deep', and all that, or maybe it is just that people who come from islands have this need to be near the water.

One of the things I always have to explain to students in North America is that Caribbean island nations are far from being homogenous. That, in fact, they are quite proud of their differences, often in contentious ways. Still, islands in the Caribbean, the Pacific and the North Atlantic do have shared characteristics. Being surrounded by water – especially in the old days before aeroplane travel – meant it was not easy to get away. That did not stop people from trying, and as a child I remember sometimes hearing stories about men stowing away in the dark holds of those big ships that docked in Kingston Harbour.

The ancestors of the majority of Jamaican people were forcibly brought to the island on big slave ships. They were captured in Africa and transported in appalling and inhumane conditions and brought as units of unpaid labour for the island's sugar plantations, and for this reason slavery has supplied the ongoing metaphor for almost all worthwhile Jamaican creative endeavours. From the Maroons – including Nanny of the Maroons about whom I write in many of my poems – who waged relentless resistance against plantation slavery, to Rastafarians who took up the fight against 'Babylon', that is, the British colonial system, Jamaican culture continually references slavery.

Jamaican musicians like Bob Marley, Peter Tosh, Bunny Wailer, Burning Spear, Culture, Ibo Cooper of Third World, Tony Rebel, Steel Pulse, Damian 'Junior Gong' Marley, Chronnixx and Queen Ifrica, all have at the heart of their project this focus on what Rastafarians call 'Truth and Right.' I think that this concern for justice is born out of an island mentality; you are there in this cut-off place, you might not be there of your own volition, but you are surrounded by the sea, marooned, so to speak, and you are going to have to stay there and actively try to work it out. I believe that is what I am also trying to do in my work.

I-Land

Being surrounded by the sea also means being constantly aware of this great force that cannot be controlled by humans. Life on an island is always punctuated by reports of people being lost to the sea. The sea is always there in the background as a force both benign and dangerous, it feeds you and it kills you and it is all around you.

6

Daffodil-bashing

OKAY, SO EVERY writer who grew up under British colonial rule has had something to say about one of the most famous poems ever written, 'I Wandered Lonely as a Cloud' aka 'The Daffodils'. And, of course, that body of musings has been read by some as constituting nothing less than a personal attack upon the great Romantic poet William Wordsworth. I have a clear and slightly frightening memory of one of the grand dames of English literature launching into a fierce scolding of a group of writers from the British Commonwealth at a conference hosted in London. Her broadside went something like this: 'THIS DAFFODIL-BASHING MUST END! YOU KNOW NOTHING, NOTHING AT ALL ABOUT WILLIAM WORDSWORTH!'

To say that we knew nothing at all about William Wordsworth was deeply condescending; and to yell at us as if we were small children simply underscored why so many writers and artists at that gathering were of the opinion that the sound colonial educations we received did not take our own opinions as thinking, feeling human beings into account. 'The Daffodils' merely symbolised that kind of imperial insensitivity: it was the one poem that every single person in the British Commonwealth had been taught, and it was about a flower that most of us had never actually seen.

But the nanny-like scolding of that British woman writer, who as I recall was partial to carrying handbags that looked as though they had been passed on to her by the Queen, set me to thinking, what exactly did I know about William Wordsworth? So, over the years I have made it my business to find out about this poet whose work has had such a powerful influence on the lives of so many people all over the world. After much reading and three visits to the Lake District, including a reading of my own poetry at Dove Cottage in 2000, I must say that there are things which I found out that have made me feel way more sympathetic to Wordsworth than I did back in the days when I needed to question why I was taught to privilege his poem about daffodils above all other poems about flowers.

This is not going to be any long defence of a poet who clearly needs no defending from the likes of me but, first of all, Wordsworth was orphaned at a very early age and he was boarded out. As a young man, he went travelling to France where he fathered a child, and he seemed to suffer from great guilt about this all through his life. He lived in rented houses. One time he had a disagreement with his landlord (or landlady) and he and his family were worried that they'd be put out of their house. His little daughter died, his son died. His beloved brother died at sea, he spoke funny, and, when he was offered the post of Poet Laureate, he declined because he did not want to have to leave the country to go to the big city (perhaps he was conscious of his Cumbrian accent, which sounds at times like Jamaican speech with that broad 'a' like in 'waaata'), where he'd have to play at being sophisticated. What I am saying is, he had his fair share of hard knocks. And he did not personally command the colonial authorities to force-feed us his poems.

He wrote poems about homeless people, people on the margins of society, like leech-gatherers and gypsies, and a magnificent poem about a Black woman exiled from France. He wrote a poem titled 'Upon Westminster Bridge' that many ordinary Jamaican people were also made to memorise in primary school, and that may, in a strange way, have helped to anchor some of them when they went as immigrants to Britain. I have heard tell of immigrants who, at their earliest opportunity, made their way into the city of London to stand on Westminster Bridge and recite that poem, and by so doing they were able to feel briefly connected to a place in which they often felt frightened, lonely and alienated.

I'm personally giving him a break from now on.

7

The groom

BY THE TIME I was about seven or eight years old I had memorised quite a few songs and poems. I believe that I recited my first poem in public when I went with my mother to a wedding. This was the same wedding where the groom asked me to sit with him and pretend that I was his little sister.

The groom was seated by himself on a straight-backed chair at the far end of a verandah where guests were gathering at about 7.30 one Saturday morning.

A morning wedding, not held in a church, a ceremony performed not by a minister but by a justice of the peace, a bride who wore a short dress with a veil that did not cover her face. Even a seven-year-old child knew something was not usual about that.

'Behave,' my mother had said. 'Sit there and behave.' And then she'd disappeared into the bedroom to help ready the bride for her entrance.

'Hello,' said the groom as I walked by him on a reconnaissance mission to see if there were any children my age at this wedding that I could play with.

'Hello, sir.'

'Guess what? I have a sister who is just about your age.'

'Where is your sister? Is she here?'

'No, I wish she was, she is in St Lucia where I'm from.'

The groom sang his words more than spoke them.

'May I see your doll? My little sister has a doll's house; I made it for her.'

I'd looked up at the groom when he said that. You could tell he was tall even though he was sitting down. He had a bony, handsome face and he was sweating hard although it was a cool December morning. He kept mopping his face with a blue handkerchief that matched his tie.

I showed him the doll. It was medium-sized with dark brown hair and amber-coloured glass eyes; the doll stared straight ahead when handed over to the groom, who admired her dress, which was a matching version of the yellow taffeta dress I was wearing.

'This is a really nice doll. Did you make her dress yourself?

'No, my mother made my dress,' I said, fanning out the pleats in my skirt. 'And she made the dolly dress too.'

'I help my little sister to dress her dolls sometimes, and sometimes I help her to put them to sleep.'

'In the dolly house that you made for her?'

'Yes. Could you do something for me?'

'I don't know, what do you want me to do?'

'Just please hold my hand for a bit. I'm nervous. I don't really know anyone here. Maybe you could just pretend you're my little sister?'

The groom

'Alright.'

And I took a seat beside him in one of the chairs set out around the edge of the verandah and let him fold my small hand with its chewed seven-year-old nails into his large left hand that was sweaty and shaking.

'How come nobody in your family came from St Lucia?'

'It's too far, and there wasn't enough time. Let me show you how far.'

The groom took a pen and a sheet of paper on which some words were written, from inside the breast pocket of his jacket. He turned the paper over, and on the blank side he drew an arc, he then filled in the islands, naming them as he drew them. He started with Jamaica, which was near Cuba, then he filled in Haiti and kept drawing a lot of smaller islands all the way down to the bottom of the paper where he said Trinidad and Tobago is located close to Venezuela. Then he showed me St Lucia, where he was from, and finally he drew in tiny Barbados off by itself, almost off the right-hand side of the paper, and he explained that there were no other islands after Barbados. He then said something I've never forgotten: 'The next stop after Barbados is, guess where?'

'I don't know I am not good at geography.'

'That's okay, I'm a teacher, I'll tell you. The next stop is Africa!'

Then he explained how it had taken days and nights to travel from St Lucia to Jamaica by boat.

After the groom had drawn the first map of the West Indies I'd ever seen, we sat there in silence while I thought about sailing to Africa from Barbados. Then one of the bride's many brothers came over to the groom and said in a gruff way, 'Your time now.'

The groom gave my hand a slight squeeze, turned and looked me full in the face and whispered, 'Thank you.'

Then he got up and walked with the bride's brother along the length of the verandah out on to the front lawn, over to where a small table draped with a crocheted cloth had been set up under a mango tree. There was a vase of lilies and a bible set out on the table and it was there, at this al fresco altar, when the bride had been led forth from her room wearing a short dress and shoulder-length veil, that my mother later described as a cocktail length gown of off-white guipure lace with a fingertip veil, that the wedding ceremony was performed.

At the reception there were many speeches, but as the groom had nobody there to speak up for him, I asked my mother if I could recite a poem. I did not tell her that I now considered myself the groom's little sister, but I stepped forward and recited Leigh Hunt's 'Abou Ben Adhem' which I'd been made to memorise at All Saints School:

> *Abou Ben Adhem (may his tribe increase!)*
> *awoke one night from a deep dream of peace,*
> *And saw, within the moonlight in his room,*
> *Making it rich, and like a lily in bloom,*
> *An angel writing in a book of gold:—*
> *Exceeding peace had made Ben Adhem bold...*

The groom stood up, and with a big smile thanked me for those 'lovely words', then he took the creased paper on which he had drawn the map of the West Indies from inside his breast pocket, and read the words he'd written about promising to take care of his beautiful bride and reassuring her family that he would do everything in his power to make her happy in their new home in St Lucia.

The groom

Years later, I overheard her mother telling someone that the marriage had not lasted. The bride and groom had gone back to St Lucia to live, but the bride had been miserable because those 'small island' people there had been so hostile to her. She'd left the marriage and taken her child with her, travelling from St Lucia back to Jamaica on a big new ship named the *Federal Palm*, one of two given by Canada to the West Indies Federation to help facilitate freedom of movement between the islands.

8

Bush your yard

THE DRIVER OF the tiny white van stopped and offered me a lift as I made my way across the shopping plaza towards the taxi stand. As soon as I had managed to climb in and wedge my body sideways in the narrow, shallow shelf of a backseat, she exchanged a knowing smile with the older woman seated next to her in the passenger seat. The older woman turned to me and said, 'You are going to live long, we were just talking about you.'

Hints. Learn to take hints, to read signs. Sometimes they are just there, right up in your face; sometimes people even tell you straight; if you choose not to believe them, then you have nobody but yourself to blame.

I'd read this in a book: say you are a houseplant, and that you are kept indoors in a small clay pot. You are watered enough, given just enough light to do your plant duty, but your roots have grown so much that they are straining against the bottom and the sides of the pot. You have gone as far as you can go as a houseplant. The only thing to be done then, is for someone to take you outside, break the clay pot (very painful) shake off your roots and plant you in an open space where you just might, given enough encouragement from rain and sunshine, grow into a gorgeous flowering tree.

They dropped me off at my gate, and the driver and her passenger sped off, no doubt immediately resuming their 'susu' (gossip) about my latest personal 'autoclaps', which is what Jamaicans call misfortune and tragedy.

I noticed that the Kingston and St Andrew Corporation had sent a work crew to cut down the overgrowth in the open lot next door. Everyone on the street had been calling them to report that the lot was becoming a health hazard, a breeding ground for mosquitoes, vermin and criminals. Now that the KSAC had finally come and bushed the lot, the owner would receive a bill in the mail.

The KSAC crew had chopped down everything in the open lot except the tree where the silver patoo lived.

Another thing that I'd read somewhere: when you hear the 'patoo' (owl) call your name you will die.

I'd been standing by the gate feeling sad and sorry for myself after the little white van drove off. With tears in my eyes I gazed over at the open lot, to see the patoo staring at me between the large heart-shaped leaves of the *Bauhinia variegata*, aka the poor man's (and woman's) orchid, also known as the mountain ebony, or camel's foot tree.

Me: 'My life is a joke, they are laughing at me because I have tried to build some sort of life for myself and I've utterly failed again. Just like the time before, and the time before that, and all the times before... What about you? Are you going to hoot and laugh at me too? Hoot and mock and call, call my name?'

Of course, the patoo said nothing. Not a 'too-whit to-who' in that gargling way of owls. It just saucer-eyed me.

I went inside and made my will. A short will.

That night I stood by the fence again. This time the owl spoke:

Patoo: 'Bush your yard.'

Me: 'What?'

Patoo: 'Bush your yard. Bush your yard. Bush your…'

Me: 'Alright, alright, I'll do it. Just don't call my name, please.'

I wrote my old life a letter giving it notice. I put a stamp of a flowering tree on it and posted it between the pages of a book of Gerard Manley Hopkins's poems. The poem it faced was 'Thou art indeed just, Lord if I contend':

Thou art indeed just, Lord, if I contend
With thee; but, sir, so what I plead is just.
Why do sinners' ways prosper? and why must
Disappointment all I endeavour end?
*   Wert Thou mine enemy, O Thou my friend,*
How wouldst thou worse, I wonder, than thou dost
Defeat, thwart me? Oh, the sots and thralls of lust
Do in spare hours more thrive than I that spend,
Sir, life upon thy cause. See banks and brakes
Now, leavèd how thick! lacèd they are again
With fretty chervil, look, and fresh wind shakes
Them; birds build – but not I build; no but strain,
Time's eunuch, and not breed one work that wakes.
Mine, O thou lord of life, send my roots rain.

As if the letter was prostrating itself before the poem, just as I was prostrating myself on the floor of my room calling over and over to the Rainsource to direct some rain to my roots.

'Only after you bush your yard,' hooted patoo.

I heard somewhere that when sea captains have to turn massive ocean liners, they have to turn and turn the wheel for some time before the ship re-positions itself and begins to head in the right direction. During this process the ship is also liable to go badly off course.

More about bushing that yard. Some seemingly healthy plants are going to go right along with the rank weeds when you bush your yard.

So bush bush. Bush here, there it all goes. Weed and flowering bush and peppermint, right along with cow itch and cerasee.

No, I can't come to breakfast or lunch or tea or dinner.

No, I don't want to talk on the telephone because you will be sifting my carefree chatter for kernels of foolishness to pop to your posse as soon as you hang up the phone.

No, I have no opinion on that matter because in the past I had a habit of thinking out loud, and many is the time that my half-digested reasonings have provided you with proof that they stopped providing Jamaicans with a good colonial education at exactly 6.45 one Monday morning; the same exact morning that I first went to school.

Nope, I'm no longer providing the meat for you to dine out on. Not the meat, not the seasoning. From now on I will confine my reasoning to my writing. Who knows, with me gone, your sharp-fanged dinner guests might even turn to chaw chawing your flesh. That's it, friends – not again – show done. Yard bushed.

'What will I be left with?' I asked patoo.

'Wait and see. Wait and see. Wait and see.'

I did not have to wait long. One morning I woke up early with the final line of Gerard Manley Hopkins's 'Thou art indeed just, Lord, if I contend' on my mind. I reached for the notebook I'd taken to keeping on the bedside table, and taking the last line as the title, I wrote:

'Mine O thou lord of life, send my roots rain'

For I have been planted long
in a sere dry place,
watered only occasionally,
with odd overflows
from a passing cloud's face.
In my morning
I imitated the bougainvillea
(in appearances
I am hybrid).
I gave forth defiant alleluias
of flowering,
covered my aridity
with red-petalled blisters
grouped close, from far
they were a borealis
of save-face-flowers.
In the middle of my life span
my trunk's not so limber
my sap flows thicker.
My region has posted signs
that speak of scarce water.
At night, God, I feel
my feet powder.
Lord, let the preying worms

Bush your yard

wait to feast in vain
In this noon of my orchard
O send me deep rain.

And one day the rains came; and the replenishing floods
descended.

9

Redemption is the key

I AM ALWAYS drawn to stories in human history in which someone is redeemed. Instances where a debt owed is cancelled, when some good soul comes forward and pays off the bond price that sets the indebted free.

As I have not found many such stories of Redemption in the history of my own people, Redemption has become my keyword, and I am hoping that in time others will join me on the Redemption train, which ideally leaves from Redemption Ground Market in the city of Kingston – once a cholera cemetery that became a market by day and a nocturnal meeting place for faith-keepers of African spirituality and foundation builders of the Rastafarian religion such as Leonard Howell and Joseph Nathaniel Hibbert.

There were women who were gathered there too, women whose names I do not know, but they were there, and engaged in the active Redemption of their people through the uncompromising rejection of mental slavery.

Many of these men and women had been followers of Alexander Bedward, the charismatic preacher who had galvanised many thousands of followers with his anti-colonial rhetoric and his promise to fly away home taking his followers with him. A redemptive move, up and away from the misery and desolation of life in post-slavery Jamaica. We will never know if he could have made good on this promise, because his career was cut short by the authorities and he ended his life in a mental institution.

But these men and women, his followers, kept on, and there on Redemption Ground they fashioned a religion with a God who looked more like them, and one day one of its followers, who was born out of the meeting of Europe and Africa, wrote a song inspired by the words of one of the world's great freedom fighters, Marcus Garvey.

The song is called 'Redemption Song', and it has become an anthem for people all over the world.

Implied in the words is the plea for us all to help to sing, to write Redemption songs; songs and stories, for the rest of my life, this is what I hope to be doing.

10

'Immortal, Invisible, God Only Wise'

As a child growing up on the island of Jamaica, it seemed to me that people, especially women, were always singing hymns as they went about their business. Women bending low over wash tubs, or standing knee deep in swift running rivers, would produce scrub rhythms from the friction of soaped cloth rubbed hard between fists; and over that wash-wash rhythm, they would moan hymns like 'What a Friend We Have in Jesus'.

Women ironing would sing too, accompanying their hymns with the thump and slide of heavy clothes irons. One especially weighty iron was known as a 'self-heater' because it had a hollow interior designed to hold hell-hot coals. Perhaps I imagined this, but the washerwomen seemed to favour hymns about sins being washed white as snow – something most Jamaicans had never witnessed first-hand – and the ironing women seemed to like hymns that lamented our trespasses and sins and the consequent fear of hell. I like to think that the island was girdled round by a kind of eremitical domestic holiness when those women sang.

On the streets of Kingston, preachers, often from Revivalist or Pocomania groups formed from the syncretisation of African and European religions, would rock out spirited versions of Christian hymns that married, as one of our philosophers Rex Nettleford said, the melodies of Europe with the rhythms of Africa. Salvation Army brass bands with their booming kettle drums contributed stirring renditions of hymns as they marched out from the Bramwell Booth Memorial Hall onto the streets of the city, there to lift up the fallen and convert the wayward.

Hymns were sung at political gatherings. 'There Were Ninety and Nine' was raised at every meeting of the People's National Party, because it was the favourite hymn of Norman Washington Manley, often called the father of modern Jamaica. Jamaicans call this hymn and others like it 'sankeys' after the powerful revival-style hymns performed by the great American Evangelist and baritone Ira D. Sankey.

Christian hymns were also routinely repurposed by Rastafarians, a religious sect who regard their main mission as the decolonisation of the minds of African-Jamaicans; so, a sankey like 'If you only knew the Blessing that Salvation brings', when sung at a Rastafarian gathering or 'reasoning', would become 'If you only knew the Blessing Rastafari brings'. Performed in a hypnotic chanting style and underscored by powerful explosive drumming, such hymns became anthems of resistance, especially when delivered in the thunderous basso profundo of the great Rastafarian elder Mortimo Planno, who was Bob Marley's spiritual advisor.

But my mother and her people were Anglicans – or, as she preferred to say, they belonged to the 'Church of England'.

Her father David, in addition to being a village lawyer, was the catechist in the local Anglican church, and so my mother and her people all grew up being entirely comfortable with the language of the Book of Common Prayer, and very familiar with the poetry of the hymns written by some of the finest poets in the English language.

My mother relied on hymns to get her through the daily rounds and numerous common tasks involved in raising nine children on very little money. She would sing these hymns in a funny out-of-breath style, opting to hum some lines low under her breath as if internalising their deeper meaning, and singing others out loud, offering them up for all to hear in bursts of lamentation, praise, petition or thanksgiving. Ironically, one of her favourite hymns, 'Immortal, Invisible, God Only Wise', was written in 1867 not by an Anglican but by a Scottish Methodist minister, Reverend W. Chalmers Smith, and it has become my favourite hymn.

I love and admire 'Immortal, Invisible, God Only Wise' mainly because it is a triumph of a praise song that uses words to describe the indescribable; something to which any hard-grafting poet can relate. It does so in what the English moral philosopher Mary Warnock calls 'beautiful unordinary language', the only language fitting to describe God who cannot be seen through mortal eyes; who is immortal, most wise, most blessed and most glorious; and above all, most worthy of the ultimate honorific: 'The Ancient of Days', who is almighty and victorious and whose great name we praise.

When I was an art student I always used to pause as I sang that opening verse and picture William Blake's fiery rendering of Urizen setting a compass to the earth; but some time ago something in me shifted, and now when I sing that line I see instead my mother, her hair gone completely white, contained in that bright circle of Blake's making, and she is measuring yards of richly brocaded fabric with her worn dressmaking tape measure.

I love, just love, what happens in the second verse of this hymn, how one of the loveliest surprises I know of in all of writing occurs. The Immortal, Invisible, who does not rest or make haste, is described as 'Silent as LIGHT'. Not night, but light. Lovely silent light which is invoked in every verse except verse number three. And then the old adage 'Waste not, want not' becomes a divine attribute of a mighty God, who does not waste nor want. Throughout this hymn, there are graceful gestures connecting the Divine to the daily in lovely numinous hints and gestures.

I sang this hymn at least a hundred times at morning assembly during the years I attended school in Jamaica. I have sung it in churches in Ann Arbor, Michigan and in Toronto and Vancouver, Canada, and at least once in Durham Cathedral in England. My husband, Ted Chamberlin, and I chose it as the hymn for our wedding, so it has a very special place in my worship life, but these days it seems to have taken on even greater significance as I watch the news and I find myself turning to the lines:

Thy justice like mountains high soaring above
Thy clouds which are fountains of goodness and love.

These words reassure me that no matter how much injustice there is in the world there is an ultimate source of justice, one that can only be measured by the heights of mountains. I am reassured, too, that there is a supply of goodness and love, which comes down from the clouds like rain or snow and, because this hymn is powered by the unordinary, this cloud-source of goodness and love paradoxically flows like a fountain.

These days, as I watch the news I feel the need to remind myself of the constant nature of the divine, that 'nought changeth', even as we mortals blossom and flourish as leaves on a tree, and then, without a doubt, wither and perish. In the original version of this hymn, the penultimate verse contains these lines, which were changed (by the Wesleys?):

But of all thy rich graces this grace, Lord, impart
Take the veil from our faces, the vile from our hearts.

I wish they had kept those words; for the graceful turn of veil into vile – a hard, but so honest word which resonates with those of us who are painfully aware that we often are, as the Book of Common Prayer says, 'Most miserable offenders.'

But mostly this is my favourite hymn because it almost succeeds in describing what no one can ever fully describe: the greatest of all mysteries that is veiled in silent light.

11

My painted skirt like a scenic 78

LYING AWAKE in bed in the room I share with my two sisters, who are both asleep, I play the game I have invented called 'Take control of the deejay over at the Loyal Levi Memorial Hall'.

The Loyal Levi Memorial Hall was a school by day – Rochdale College run by Mr Tingling and Miss Burton – a Lodge Hall by night, and a dance hall on weekends and public holidays. All over the city of Kingston there used to be such multipurpose halls, and all over the city such places were filled with dance fans come Saturday night.

I take control of the deejay from the comfort and safety of my bed because I am not old enough to go dancing, but I have done this before on other Saturday nights, I know what to do. I whisper into the dark: 'Alright now, play "Sea Cruise" by Frankie Ford.'

There is a pause as my command skips over several sets of rooftops then drops down and penetrates into the mind of the deejay. Then there is the scratching sound of the needle on the broad-faced 78 rpm record followed by a musical churning as a love boat engine stirs up the waters of rhythm.

Once I get the attention of the deejay, he often plays what I tell him for up to seven or eight songs in a row. So, after Frankie Ford sails away, I command, command Professor Longhair of New Orleans to plead: 'Baby, Let Me Hold Your Hand'.

And after that I want, no I need, I must and am bound to hear Huey 'Piano' Smith tell how he has 'High Blood Pressure'. That one is my favourite.

I love it so much that I cannot stay in my bed, so I project myself through the window and go flying over the rooftops where I hover, O yeah, and then land feet first as a 'Bony Maroni' dancing girl in the midst of a crowded dance floor.

I am wearing five yards of swing skirt. A hand-painted skirt, covered with scenes of Jamaica skilfully rendered by some gifted local artist. Around the hem of my skirt, cobalt-blue waves lap at calico white sands. The Blue Mountains peak near my waist. Dunn's River Falls cascades from my left hip, a scarlet hibiscus blooms over my navel and streamer-tailed humming birds hover around my knees. Up my right thigh rises a tall and stately coconut tree. My blouse is allamanda-yellow, it has a standing-collar and is sleeveless. My fabulous outfit is completed by brand new size five ackee-seed black ballet shoes.

I have come to dance. I can spin and spin and execute that cute shuffle when I complete the whirling circle that gives me the needed momentum to push off and spin again.

Dancing girls like me spin from when the music starts till it ends. My dancing partner's function is solely to push me gently out and pull me in again, then to grasp me suddenly, fiercely around my waist to remind me that I do not dance alone. Every time I spin, the five yards of my skirt float out till I look like a scenic 78 record spinning.

And I instruct the deejay: play Jamaican music now. Strictly yard. Play 'Boogie Rock' by Laurel Aitken. Let my people's voices ride the soundwaves right there alongside Jim Reeves and Marty Robbins, Frankie Laine and Patti Page.

May I pause a minute here to say that I never did like Patti Page's water cracker singing? That I myself would not give her even a ha'penny for that doggie in the window?

Anyway, I tell the deejay, play 'Little Vilma' by the Blues Busters. Lloydie and Boasie, those two fine Black princes come from Montego Bay, with their strong singing and their flawless harmonising. Play them, Mr Deejay!

Play Wilfred Jackie Edwards – what a man smooth! Play 'Tell Me Darling' and play Keith and Enid, who are worried, 'Worried Over You'.

Play 'Muriel' by Alton and Eddy. Strictly local, this. Play what I tell you.

And after this grand sweep of lyrical nationalism please play for me the fabulous singing ladies, the ones whose voices I'll want to conjure when I come one day to accept that I am a poet.

Mr Deejay please play LaVern Baker singing her praise song to that most able of men, 'Jim Dandy'.

Play Sarah Vaughan, of the wondrous voice and the gorgeous slipper satin evening gowns, make her sing me a 'Lullaby of Birdland'.

Play enchantress Dinah Washington, let her spirit guide me through the isle of joy that is Manhattan.

And play any song by the high priestess Nina Simone. For when I come to write, if I can write like Nina sings... Oh, if I could only write like Nina sings 'Little Girl Blue'.

Play for me those ladies with voices, coloratura like Myers rum and strong Machado tobacco, mysterious as the insides of nightclubs named Blue Note and Smoky Places.

Then play Ella of the crystalline clean baptismal soul-rinse singing.

This is how I play the game until I fall asleep to Dakota Staton crooning about how it all started at *The Late Late Show*.

12

The Caribbean imaginary, for Ifeona Fulani

THE POEM 'Guinea Woman' (p.30) was born out of a strong need to honour my maternal great grandmother who would have been a small child when slavery was abolished in 1838.

All I knew of her when I wrote the poem was that she was very dark-skinned, and that people called her a Guinea woman because of the small warts across the top of her cheeks. I also knew that she had had my mother's mother with an Irish man, and that later in her life she married a man of African descent. That was almost all I knew about her then. Most of the poem is therefore my imagining.

There were no family photographs of her. There were no archives to visit, no ancestry dot.com that kept records of the lives of people like my great grandmother, and so I learnt early in my life as a writer that if I wanted to write about my people I had to learn to listen carefully to family stories then imagine, and constantly reimagine those stories. And that is because, in the Caribbean, the centre will not, does not, and looks like it might not ever, hold. A Caribbean writer therefore has to take what is available even if much has been lost, and give it a presence, a reality through their imagination.

All writers do this, but Caribbean writers face formidable or particular challenges because of the ways in which slavery, and then colonialism, erased or distorted so much of our lives that we have had to learn to write ourselves into the story in any way we can.

'Quest'

At aged twelve, six days
into the start of a year
this girl was seated

in a whitewashed classroom
dreaming herself outdoors
and up Lignum vitae trees

and heard a teacher read:
'A cold coming we had of it'
and just so went on a journey

with men whose names
or what they were in search of
never revealed.

She only recalls that when
a prefect rang the lunch bell
she was wrenched from the ride
with the men on a quest.
And that she tested on her tongue
the words refractory

and silken as adjectives for herself,
as hints for her own journey:
Girl exited room with vaulted ceiling, disoriented.

The feeling of being lost is still very much part of all our experience and I never thought I'd live to say this, but it's not all bad, and it has a history that goes back well before our modern times.

The word 'disoriented', which we often use to describe how we feel when we're not sure where we are, was first coined centuries ago to describe the experience of venturing far from a centre of certainties.

For medieval Christian, Jewish and Islamic sailors who went out from the Mediterranean onto the Atlantic Ocean, that centre was in the east, the Orient, where they all identified their spiritual and their secular home. If they ventured too far into the western sea – which they often did – it was said that they would become '<u>dis</u>-oriented', alienated from their home.

Being disoriented has negative connotations for many of us, and especially for those in the Caribbean who feel far from their ancestral home in Africa or India; but on the positive side it is nothing more – or less – than not being sure about things and being surprised by new things, and that is what Caribbean literature has often taken as its mandate, making a virtue out of necessity.

I lost all the books I collected for over thirty years, most of the paintings I'd done, and many photographs and cherished objects, to Hurricane Gilbert. I have had to learn to re-imagine my relationship with lost things.

And other forces come into play. The primary school that I attended, the very good school where I was made to memorise dozens of poems, mostly by the British Romantic poets, a school that helped to nourish my earliest interest in poetry, was one day bulldozed to the ground. I have never been able to figure out why.

I periodically reimagine my lost paintings. I reimagine my old school. My father died when I was fifteen, I often imagine what life for my family would have been like had he lived.

My memoir *From Harvey River* was born out of a need to preserve a time and a place that is all but gone, because the small village founded by my paternal great grandfather looks nothing like it did in my mother's time, the family home no longer exists, and climate change has altered the flow of the river. I had to imagine it in all its original bucolic charm in order to write that memoir.

And I do this because as a Caribbean writer it is my job to imagine and keep reimagining the past and the future into being, so that the best of what was lost might exist again in the future.

13

A meditation on friendships past

I ONCE HEARD a story about a man – I heard it from a friend of his who was no longer a friend – who got up in the middle of a dinner party where there was much good food and wine and witty conversation and said something to the effect that he was not going to spend his time like that any more. I imagined that he just put down his knife and fork and declared that he was going to find something better to do with his life than being a charming guest at dinner parties, and he did. He went on to research and write a powerful and well-received book about homeless children, but he lost quite a few friends after that dinner party.

Let me tell you about another dinner party, one where I was the hostess. It was in the mid-1970s in Kingston, Jamaica. I was then newly married to a man who was a popular radio announcer. Our mutual interest in a wide range of music had brought us together; sadly, it was not enough to keep us together. One of the benefits of that relationship was that

I went with him to many music concerts in Jamaica and the USA; and I sometimes found myself in the company of singers and musicians and major players in the music industry including Miriam Makeba, Marvin Gaye, Bob Marley, Les McCann, the Four Tops, Roberta Flack, and the Staple Singers. Mavis Staples I especially remember, because she solved the problem of remembering people's names by calling everybody – man, woman and child – 'Montana'. I met the Staple Singers when they appeared as the other half of the bill with Les McCann, who had just produced the amazing *First Take* album with Roberta Flack.

The night the show opened, the entire band, along with the promoter of the show, a famous New York DJ named Ed Williams, came to dinner at our house. The food was plentiful – good Jamaican food: escoveitched fish, fricassee chicken, curried goat, rice and peas, and fried plantain. Good wine and every other kind of liquor flowed. I was a charming hostess, laughing merrily, making witty remarks to beat the band as I saw that everyone was fed and watered. Les McCann is a big man, who enjoys his food (I know that because at the end of the evening he told me so). He also said something else, he said: 'It must be very difficult for you to keep pretending that you are not as bright as you are.'

In those days I worked as an advertising copywriter, and for that reason I can identify fully with Peggy Olson, that character on the TV show *Mad Men*, for I too was often the only female member of the creative team and I too (at the risk of sounding self-aggrandising) was very good at my job. I wrote radio and television commercials, one of which won a Clio prize (advertising's Oscars). After I sat my A-levels and finished school, I worked for a year as a junior bookmobile librarian, then as a trainee copywriter in an advertising agency. I left that job to go and study art at the Jamaica School of Art and then at The Art Students League of New York. I'd come back to Jamaica and taught art and some creative writing at Jamaica College, then I'd gone back to working as an advertising copywriter; mostly because the pay was better and because I got to work in a fancy office with exciting, interesting people. I had no life plan, nor any clear idea of who or what I wanted to be in those days, so as the fabulous writer Grace Paley, whom I met at the University of Michigan, once said, I just kept doing 'the next thing'.

No matter what I was doing, I was also writing poems, but I never imagined that I was doing anything of great significance.

Most people would have considered me extremely lucky, at the age of twenty-five, to be married, living in a fine townhouse, and doing well at my job where I got to write and produce press, radio and TV commercials, and travel abroad to Miami, London and Toronto. I imagined that I was keeping my interest in the arts alive when I wrote and produced commercials with Olive Lewin and the Jamaica Folk Singers for Horlicks and worked with Tony Gambrill to produce radio and TV ads for Dragon Stout featuring the daddy of all deejays and rappers, U-Roy. I was sure that I was doing my civic duty when I wrote and produced radio and television ads for the Jamaica Family Planning Association. I had a fine life. Why was I so deep to the marrow unhappy?

A year after Les McCann said what he said to me at that dinner party, I started to make changes in my life. While my decision to – as the man at the dinner party at the beginning of this essay said – not spend my time like that any more did not happen as suddenly, or so dramatically, I did have a clear moment of decision which occurred, of all places, in the ladies' room at the Bottom Line jazz club in New York.

I was in the company of my then husband and some other interesting people including a few writers, and we had come to hear Les McCann perform; but first we had to sit through an opening act by a woman whose claim to fame was that she had been one of Miles Davis's several wives.

At some point during her on-stage carryings on, I got up and went to the ladies' room to get away from what was making my head hurt.

I looked at myself in the mirror of the ladies' room in the Bottom Line club in New York City on that August night in 1974 and I said to myself, 'You have got to change your life,' and then I started to cry. At least four or five women came and went as I stood there off to the side of the sink weeping, but I do not recall any of them asking me what the matter was or if they could help in any way. Maybe the sight of a woman crying in a bathroom in a nightclub in New York City was not all that unusual.

I stood there alone with tears running down my face, dressed from head to toe in sleek black as if somebody had just died. After a while I managed to pull myself together enough to wash my face, put on some lipstick and go back inside.

'Good timing, she finished her set while you were in there.'

'Thank God for that. I need a cigarette, I'm going outside.'

Standing outside in the late summer evening I smoked a shocking-pink Balkan Sobranie. I had been introduced to these strong, brightly coloured cigarettes on my first visit to London, and I'd been glad to find them in a tobacconist in Manhattan earlier that evening. I believed that they looked cool against the all-black outfits I had taken to wearing.

A meditation on friendships past

As trite as this sounds, I love New York, especially in the autumn, and this was a late August night, just a little cool, and I could smell and feel the season about to shift.

'You have got to change your life,' I'd said to myself in the mirror back there in the ladies' room, although I doubt that I had then read Rilke's great poem 'Archaic Torso of Apollo', which concludes with that same line. The poet had been moved by the power and beauty of an ancient statue. I had been moved from my comfortable seat by a woman whose performance was making me conscious of the fact that my own artistic talents were urgently crying out to be expressed. When I said goodbye to the people I was with at the end of that evening, I knew that I'd never see any of them again. A year later I left that marriage under less than ideal circumstances and began to do more of my own writing and painting.

'WHAT MORE could you want?' someone once asked me. What more could I want? At the time, I was trying to make a living as a writer and teacher of poetry and I was a single mother raising my beloved son Miles. There was a lot more for me to want.

I have become convinced over time that I have every right to want to do more of the work I believe I have been given to do. At this stage of my life, I do not now regret one day that I have spent working at any job, because somehow every job that I have ever had has always fed and nourished my writing. A good example of the way in which things have worked together for the good is something that happened when I worked at McCann Erickson (where the late Edgar Stewart gave me the opportunity to go for training in the London office). It was while I was working at their office in

Kingston that one of the most important breaks in my life as a poet came to me.

Everybody there knew that I wrote poetry. Sometimes, when I was tired of coming up with new concepts and catchy slogans for anything from motor cars to tinned beef and fine jewellery, I'd announce to the creative director, an extremely talented African American man named Joe Grey who would sometimes close his office door and play his trumpet when he needed inspiration, that I was shutting my door because I needed to clear my head. He understood that that meant I was working on my poems.

One day Ralph Shearer, who was then the head of the production department, came to me and said, 'I'm designing the *Jamaica Journal*, why don't you give me some of your poems to show to the editor?' I did, and he came back after a few weeks and said, 'They liked the poems and the head of the institute says he wants to see you.' So, one day during my lunch hour, I went down to the Institute of Jamaica where I was shown into the office of Neville Dawes, the then director, and he looked at me gravely and said, 'Do you know that you're a poet?'

I believe that you cannot just decide that you're a poet.

When I was fifteen years old, my English teacher, Lena Robinson Aub, had told me that I was a writer. Lena Robinson Aub was a very confident English woman who had read English at Oxford, and she helped to cultivate my love of English literature from Chaucer to Shakespeare's history plays to the social realism or kitchen sink school of writers like Lynne Reid Banks, John Braine and Alan Sillitoe.

It was Lena Robinson Aub who had told me, in her straightforward way, after I'd complained to her that I wanted to read a book with a character who looked and sounded more like me, that I was a writer, and that I should write what I wanted to read.

When I'd first started to write poems I never told anyone what I was doing. It was my secret and my way of coping with the tidal waves of feelings that had often pulled me down into sink holes of adolescent sadness. But I had no idea what to do with these poetic offerings once they'd arrived, so I once made a funeral pyre of all my writings in the back yard and burnt them, every one. But they still insisted on coming. One day I decided to just accept the fact that I was and am, by some great grace, a poet, but that poetry was something I would do in private without any expectation of reward or recognition.

And here I return to where I started. I have noticed that some people who were happy to be my friend when I was an advertising copywriter who was also a sometime painter and art teacher, were not so happy once I openly began to lay claim to being a poet.

But as my dear friend the brilliant historian, poet and nation-builder Sir Philip Sherlock – who is my absolute favourite Jamaican poet – would say: 'Some of us come in by the tradespersons' entrance, nothing wrong with that.'

In any case, from all I've read and heard, some of the most unlikely people have been given the gift of poetry. Poetry seems to like to go its own way, keeping its own 'leggo beast' company with whomever it pleases. Hence all sorts of upstarts and 'unsuitable' people – Shakespeare being chief amongst them – are poets.

I also realised that a big part of my initial reluctance to fully embrace my gifts was that I always feared that it would bring great upheaval and uncertainty to my life. Boy, was I ever right.

I had to leave my first marriage, become estranged from my family for a time, and to make what in retrospect now seems like a series of quite reckless, unwise, inexplicably lonely and alienating life choices; but somehow, from where I now stand, it all seems to have worked together for good.

I remember once speaking aloud, presumably to poetry, and saying something like 'Okay, I'll go along with this business of being a poet on one condition. I want to grow, to develop to be the best that I can be at this. Now do what you want to do with me.'

14

Hurricanes

June too soon,
July stand by,
August look out you must,
September remember,
October all over.

I WAS ONLY four years old, but I remember that my mother put my one-week-old baby brother Nigel in the bottom drawer of the bureau. She said it was to protect him in case we lost our roof.

I remember my whole family – my mother and father and my eight siblings Barbara, Howard, Carmen, Bunny, Kingsley and Karl the twins, Keith, Nigel and me all huddled together in our house, which under normal circumstances would have been described as 'cramped', but with a hurricane raging outside felt safe, warm and cosy.

It was August 1951 and Hurricane Charlie was about to prove what we all believed at the time to be true: that a man hurricane – that is, a hurricane named after a man – was badder than one named for a woman.

Charlie proceeded to rain hard and heavy blows on the island of Jamaica. It had made landfall during the night of August 17th and quickly moved across the island, beating down everything in its path as it went. Some time during the morning of August 18th, the wicked winds and torrential rain suddenly stopped. 'This is just the eye of the hurricane,' my father explained, as the curious stillness descended, 'Charlie will be coming back.' Then he opened the front door and allowed my older siblings out into the yard to splash about in the deep rainwater pool that had collected outside.

Just as suddenly as it had stopped, the wind started up again, announcing its return through weird whistling noises and a frantic stirring of the waters of what had become a big wading pool in which tree branches and fallen fruit bobbed about. Soaked to the skin and deliriously happy, my siblings dashed inside and changed out of their wet clothes while my father bolted the front door shut with a wide heavy plank of wood dropped into two iron hooks set on either of the doorframe. During the calm of the eye, my mother had managed to brew up a big pot of Fry's cocoa, which we drank as we ate big thick slices of hard dough bread with butter and bully beef. We settled in again, bellies full, just in time. Charlie, it seemed, had rested enough and was returning with more brute force and power than before. By the time he left, there were 152 people dead and 2,000 homeless.

'June too soon, July stand by, August look out you must, September remember, October all over' is what they taught us in primary school about hurricane season. We believed this, and come September we expected to look back and remember, and when October came around, the people of the Caribbean would all breathe a sigh of relief, expecting to feel safe for another year because hurricane season was all over. And then came Gilbert. 'Wild Gilbert', as one of our finest lyricists, Lloyd Lovindeer, christened the hurricane that battered down Jamaica in September 1988.

In between Charlie and Gilbert, Jamaica had experienced a number of storms, including Hurricane Hazel. Hazel did not do as much damage to Jamaica as Charlie, but she did manage to travel further, becoming more un-ladylike and virago-ish as she went. She did serious damage in upstate New York and killed several people in Ontario, Canada. Up until Gilbert, the island of Jamaica had been miraculously spared from a full-impact hurricane. Sure, we'd had storms, 'breeze-blow' and torrential rains that caused loss of life, washed away houses and livestock and reconfigured parts of the island's landscape, but we'd not seen anything like Gilbert – well, not since Charlie.

The 'razor blade winds', my son Miles, who was then eight years old, called them. A perfect description for the winds of Gilbert which, when they started up on the morning of September 12th, immediately set about decapitating trees and mincing the leaves into green confetti which they then sprayed with brute force onto any standing surface. The effect was very artistic, a form of pointillism: walls densely stippled with green vegetable matter. The only problem was, this verdant patina was being created on the walls both outside and inside our house.

Gilbert came in the whirlwind, accompanied by torrential waterfalls of rain – hard rain sheeting down. We were huddled safe and dry inside, marvelling at the ferocity of the wind and rain, the lightning and the thunder, when with a terrible groaning sound the roof of our house just lifted off and took flight. Suddenly there was no difference between being inside and being outside.

Gilbert rained down over my beds and chairs and tables, all over my books, all over my paintings and photographs and clothes and shoes, all over my son Miles's books and toys; almost everything we owned and treasured was soaked right through.

When the eye of the storm came we headed out and found refuge with my sister and her husband, whose roof was mercifully still intact, and we waited out the rest of Gilbert there. 'They should have called it "Roofus", not Gilbert,' said Jamaicans, who can always manage to make a joke under the worst circumstances. In the days after Gilbert, the days without electricity and running water, the island struggled to right itself again. With more than forty-five people killed, thousands left homeless and many, many thousands left roofless, I began to think more and more about how small and powerless we human beings are in the face of the Charlies and Hazels and Gilberts that are visited upon us as part of regular life in the Caribbean.

I began to wonder too if giving a hurricane a human name is necessarily a good idea. Anyone who has lived through a Hazel or a Gilbert or a Charlie must acknowledge that no human power is faintly equal to the primal force and might of a hurricane. Maybe we should just concede supremacy to hurricanes and give them numbers, or, if we insist on giving them human names, at least call them after great warriors like Muhammad Ali or Joe Louis or Nanny of the Maroons.

Strangely enough, the loss of most of my material possessions after Gilbert passed through freed me to take up opportunities to work and eventually live outside of Jamaica, and for this mixed blessing I will be always grateful. I was not in Jamaica for Hurricane Dean, but my husband and I must have made twenty telephone calls to my son, to my siblings, to friends who all mercifully came through unharmed. 'The eye missed us,' they said, 'or it would have been much worse ... but remember, the hurricane season isn't over yet.'

The people of the Caribbean have had to come to terms with the fact that the mnemonic about September remember, October all over does not hold any more. We've also had to concede that a woman hurricane – Katrina – can do more damage than any man hurricane, and that there is nothing like a hurricane, named after a man or a woman, to remind you of your own human frailty, to make you grateful when the terrible eye happens to look away from you and your loved ones.

15

For Derek Walcott

I OWE DEREK. He told me I was a poet and I knew I could believe him because nobody who knew him can truthfully say they ever heard him pay a false compliment to an aspiring writer.

In fact, the opposite was true: his standards were so exacting and his critiques so uncompromising, and he set the bar for poetry so high, that everyone coming after him will have to do – as old time Jamaicans say — 'their endeavour best'. He was the best.

He was a poet-playwright who lived for poetry, and he was born into a community that seemed to have been waiting for his coming, because his gifts were whole-heartedly embraced by St Lucians from the time he first published his verse as a schoolboy. He reciprocated by writing his people into literature. He never tired of praising St Lucia, the Helen of the Caribbean, and because he was proud of being a Caribbean man he exalted and lamented all things Caribbean: our wretched history, our perplexing present, our abiding beauty.

Derek was all about beauty. The entire body of his work can be read as a deep and wide engagement with beauty in all its manifestations.

He made ordinary St Lucian fishermen the subject of great myths.

He gave a simple Black woman sitting on a bus in Castries earrings of good gold – he stipulated that it had to be good gold – and likened her to Delacroix's *Liberty Leading the People*. He called her Beauty, and he declared that Beauty is the light of the world.

And Derek's poems are a constant source of enlightenment, wonder and delight. No modern poet ever handled the English language with more authority, skill and mastery, but he was also a very playful poet and I often engage in a game with myself in which I try to spot some of the many joyful little 'signatures' with which he marked his work.

I like his deft deployment of citrus fruit like lemons and tangerines to stimulate the sight, smell, touch and taste senses of the reader. I treasure his outrageous puns: a figment of the imagination, the banana of the mind – people from the eastern Caribbean call bananas 'figs'. My husband, Ted Chamberlin, who brokered the deal that got Derek's papers for the Thomas Fisher Rare Book Library at the University of Toronto, and who drove said papers from Boston to Toronto for twelve straight hours with only brief stops for fear one draft of a poem be lost, always says that his favourite pun in all of English literature is 'An adamant Eve'. I admire Derek's bad jokes. O, how we will miss his outrageous loud-laugh jokes, but when the phrase 'the light of the world' comes up in his poems as a quotation, as a title, in English or in Latin, '*lux mundi*', I always feel as if he wants me to bow my head in prayer.

If I'd seen him one more time, I'd intended to ask him if he thought that by writing so much about the light of the world he was doing his part in keeping encroaching darkness at bay, but I know he'd never answer a question like that, he'd expect me to figure it out for myself, and to do my part in keeping the light project going.

He was my friend. He was famously difficult; but he could also be amazingly considerate and sensitive. He was blessed with the love and devotion of extraordinary women like Margaret, and for the last half of his life the amazing Sigrid. He loved family. Anyone who ever saw him in the company of his children, Peter, Anna and Lizzie, and grandchildren could see that he held them close with a fierce and all-protecting 'hoops of steel' love.

He gave me my first creative writing lesson, and to this day I tend to look at some poems, if not through his eyes, with the awareness that he might be looking over my shoulder. I already miss him. In the over fifty years that I knew him, he gave me some of the best advice anyone has ever given me about poetry, and about life. He once insisted that I go with him and Sigrid to a gathering in Atlanta to meet Josef Brodsky. He introduced me to the great Russian by saying, 'Josef meet Lorna. She's a poet.' I still feel obliged to try to live up to that introduction. I miss him already. I will always miss him.

16

Native(s) with the warmth

As MY COUSIN Joan Moran lay dying in a hospital bed in Calgary, Alberta in the summer of the year 2001, I would sometimes fly from Toronto, where I'd moved the year before, to sit by her bedside. If she was well enough, we'd tell each other jokes and stories as we'd done ever since we were small girls, and we would remember the good old days when we were teenagers and mad over Elvis Presley.

When she came up from Lucea, Hanover to spend summer holidays with us in Kingston, my cousin Joan and I would always go to Saturday afternoon matinees at the Carib Theatre, and our joy would be complete if there happened to be an Elvis Presley movie showing, like *Jailhouse Rock* or *Blue Hawaii* or *King Creole*. We bought magazines like *Photoplay* that carried stories about Elvis, his life in the army, his marriage to Priscilla, and we'd sing along to his songs when they came on the radio. When Joan went back to Lucea we would write to each other, and she once wrote me a letter that described how she had been swooning over an Elvis Presley song playing on the radio when our Aunt Cleodine, who was a stern model of Victorian propriety, declared, 'I am sick and tired of your stupid giggling behaviour over this man Willess Bessley!'

My one consolation is that I now laugh at that joke with my cousin Myrna, Joan's sister, who looked after Joan in the last days of her life with amazing loving kindness and tender mercies, while at the same time she was taking care of her mother, my beloved Aunt Ann who died, maybe of a broken heart, a year after losing Joan who was her youngest child. I just want to put on record here that Myrna is a kind of saint.

My visits with Joan in the hospital are now all a blur and I still tear up at the thought that I won't see my beautiful cousin ever again on this earth.

When she wasn't up to chatting and making jokes I'd sit by Joan's bed and read out loud to her, sometimes from the Book of Common Prayer – my mother's people are big on The Book of Common Prayer – perhaps even more so than the Bible, except for the psalms. Number 139 which begins, 'O Lord, thou hast searched me, and known me,' was Joan's psalm of choice.

But my cousin also liked me to read poetry, especially the poetry of John Keats, and one of the things she willed to me was her book of Keats's poems and letters with her notes in the margins. In her elegant handwriting, in dark green ink, on a narrow strip of light green notepaper she wrote:

Keats is the Romantic poet who looks outward –
to grasp the true reality of the human situation.
He is the most detached of the poets –
he sees the importance of the distanced perspective.

And then she wrote:

Negative capability – the ability to step outside himself.

One of Joan's very favourite John Keats poems was 'What the Thrush Said':

O Thou, whose only book has been the light
Of supreme darkness which thou feddest on
Night after night when Phoebus was away,
To thee the Spring shall be a triple morn.
O fret not after knowledge—I have none,
And yet my song comes native with the warmth...

'We are from Jamaica, we are natives with the warmth,' my cousin and I would joke; and I'd say, '[I] Fret not after knowledge, for I have none.' And after that she would sometimes just fall asleep smiling.

17

A vulgar upstart
with 'no right to aspire to poetry'

A BRITISH CRITIC once said that about John Keats. It is safe to say that his judgment was as accurate as that of the music teacher who informed Ray Charles that he could not sing. But I've always been fascinated by the phrase: 'with no right to aspire to poetry.'

I recently heard of an academic who vehemently expressed the opinion that only the learned have the right to express their views on the poetry of John Keats, a poet whose work received some pretty savage reviews from critics in his time, and who, as I understand it, never used to be considered a 'difficult poet', like Gerard Manley Hopkins or John Milton. Difficult poet he may not be, but the Cockney Keats is possibly one of the most beloved of poets, and he is the one to whom many people feel directly connected. Most people who love Keats's poetry have at least one poem of his that they experience 'on the pulse', a poem that they feel speaks to them directly.

My experience with Keats began at the all-girls school I attended in Jamaica where I once had the distinction of collecting seventeen demerits during the course of a single term. Demerits were handed out for various infractions from insubordination to 'daydreaming', and I am certain-sure that I must have collected more demerits for 'daydreaming' than any other student who ever passed through the gates of that school. Twinned, in pairs. Coupled, in couplets. And whether they were given for 'inattentiveness', 'carelessness' or if the truth be told 'just not fitting in', I was always being punished for the flights of imagination that would often set my mind to wandering away from the classroom, past the netball court, across the playing fields, and up into the top branches of one of the many *Lignum vitae* trees covered in mauve blossoms that used to grow on the grounds. Once up there I'd sit and stare from a higher vantage point than my viewless seat in the back of the classroom. Almost invariably I would be called down from my daydreamer's perch in the *Lignum vitae* tree by a teacher awarding me a demerit or two. It was in my A level English literature paper that I first encountered the image of another daydreamer in 'To Autumn' by John Keats.

When I read it through, I just sat there and cried. I didn't know why, but I now believe that, as Rastafarians say, I 'sight up', for there in autumn, personified as a daydreaming voluptuary, I saw myself.

Sometimes whoever seeks abroad may find
Thee sitting careless on a granary floor,
Thy hair soft-lifted by the winnowing wind;

Or on a half-reap'd furrow sound asleep,
Drows'd with the fume of poppies, while thy hook
Spares the next swath and all its twinèd flowers:
And sometimes like a gleaner thou dost keep
Steady thy laden head across a brook;
Or by a cyder-press with patient look,
Thou watchest the last oozings hours by hours.

I immediately identified with this poet who reassured me
that dreamers are of value too.

Where are the songs of Spring? Ay, where are they?
Think not of them, thou hast thy music too...

Many years later when I found myself teaching an
Introduction to Poetry course at the University of Michigan,
I had a student whose parents (both academics) were going
through a bitter divorce. She came to my office one day to
tell me that the only way that she had been able to survive
what for her had been a devastating experience was by
papering a wall in her bedroom with the John Keats poems
we had read and examined in class. My student said she
often woke up late at night just to read and be sustained by
Keats's medicinal words. Her favourite poem was 'Bright
star, would I were stedfast as thou art'.

Keats must be the poet you get up and read in the middle
of the night, because I too have risen at 3 and 4am, struggled
up out of deep sleep just to read his great Odes. I did this
many times after my cousin's death and during the twelve
years that it took me to write *From Harvey River*, a memoir
of my mother and her people. Something in me wanted
to write a praise song to my people, my blood relations as

well as the people of Jamaica, but the writing of that book proved to be a long and difficult process. I experienced numerous false starts and setbacks before the very beautiful Ellen Seligman – Peace be upon her – at McClelland and Stewart accepted the manuscript and said, 'I want to be the one who brings this book home.' And God Bless her, she did. But during those years of uncertainty as to whether the book would ever become a book, I thought much about potential not being realised, about the frustration of what Keats called, in 'Ode on a Grecian Urn', 'winning near the goal'. But I also just drew great comfort and consolation from reading Keats's poems mainly because John Keats is all about truth and beauty. He, more than any other writer, has caused me to think long and hard about the love of what is true and beautiful, and how the Creator of all things seen and unseen, who bestows such gifts, is obviously totally impartial, because some of the most unlikely people have been given this gift.

But Keats is the one who wrote that a great poet has no personality. It took just such a writer to be able to rise up and fly with the song of a nightingale for eight exquisite stanzas. A writer whose sympathetic imagination could completely identify with the most beautiful and faithful of exiles, the widow Ruth who refused to abandon her own widowed mother-in-law and followed her instead to Bethlehem where their impoverished circumstances found her gleaning in a foreign field, where she heard the song of the nightingale:

Perhaps the self-same song that found a path
Through the sad heart of Ruth, when, sick for home,
She stood in tears amid the alien corn...

I have, on occasion, been reduced to tears while reading those words in a winter classroom in blessed Ann Arbor where for over twenty years I found a home at the University of Michigan, in a supportive community of people like Bob Weisbuch, Lemuel Johnson, Lincoln Faller, Sidonie Smith, Michael Schoenfeldt, George Bornstein, Laurence Goldstein, Tish O'Dowd, Thomas Toon, Nick Delbanco, Linda Gregerson, Keith Taylor, Doug Trevor, Paul Barron, Michael Byers, Marion Johnson, John Whittier-Ferguson, Theresa Tinkle, Eileen Pollack, James Jackson, Lester Monts, Michael Awkward, Evans Young, Derek Collins, Tiya Miles, Frieda Ekotto, Elizabeth James, Arlene Kizer, the two people I think of as my Ann Arbor family – Kate and Ed West – and all the others at the University of Michigan who are true lovers of poetry.

I believe that 'Ode to a Nightingale' is quite possibly the best poem that has ever been written by anybody. It is a poem with universal appeal, for who has not heard the song of a bird and wanted to rise up and fly away with it, leaving behind life's weariness, fever and fret? To fly so high that your ordinary eyesight is of no help and you to have to be piloted by your other senses.

> *I cannot see what flowers are at my feet,*
> *Nor what soft incense hangs upon the boughs,*
> *But, in embalmed darkness, guess each sweet*
> *Wherewith the seasonable month endows.*

I believe that this guessing at the sweet in the state of 'embalmed darkness,' is a way of describing faith in a fresh and moving way; and there is no one more qualified to speak on this subject than that fine young man who had to endure so much suffering and loss during his own short lifetime.

In 2013 I was fortunate enough to take part in a poetry reading at Keats House in London that was hosted by Judith Chernaik to celebrate thirty years of Poems on the Underground. I kept hoping all the time I was there that Keats, who was big on the supernatural, would show himself to me in some way, and I guess he did, because it was a truly beautiful evening.

Keats, like Ray Charles and Bob Marley and Mahalia Jackson and John Dunkley, came 'native with the warmth', and they were all in their own way vulgar upstarts with no right to aspire to poetry and music and painting. Which is why, whosoever will, without permission from Babylon's gatekeepers, can profit from the great riches they have brought forth, like the leaves of the tree of life.

'If poetry comes not as naturally as the leaves to a tree, it had better not come at all,' wrote the sweet boy about the writing of poetry for the benefit of all lovers of truth and beauty – including and especially my dear departed cousin Joan Moran – everywhere.

18

For Lee Jenkins – Cork

IN MY POEM 'Guinea Woman' (p.30) there is a sailor whose ship sailed without him from Lucea Harbour. The sailor was named George O'Brian Wilson; he was my maternal great grandfather, and he was an Irishman. He was probably Scots-Irish, because he named my grandmother Margaret Aberdeen Wilson.

The Jump Ship Irishman
who took that Guinea girl
would croon when rum
anointed his tongue

And she left to mind
first mulatta child
would go at end of day
to ululate by the Bay

For Lee Jenkins – Cork

I am O'Rahailly, he croons
She moans, Since them
carry mi from Guinea
mi can't go home.

Of crossover griot
they want to know
how all this come about?
to no known answer.

Still they ask her
why you chant so?
And why she turn poet
not even she know.

If you want to know exactly when my great grandfather landed on the island of Jamaica, if you want dates and time and proof as to where exactly he came from – provenance, provenance – I'd tell you if I knew.

But he himself was a man who deemed it fit to inform no one from whence he'd come, and why he would never return there.

Except when sprung by spirits he'd be at home in the Gaelic tongue, O such a torrential singing.

According to family lore, George O'Brian Wilson jumped ship. Maybe he just slipped over the side and swam into Lucea Harbour some time during the second half of the nineteenth century and assumed a different life. He was a survivor.

The family thinks he may have been from Galway, but for all I know he could have been a jump ship sailor from Cork.

'Song of the Jump Ship Sailor'

I am from Cork, he said, so I peeled off that barque
easy as you please,

rolled into the night sea, and rode the white horses
into Lucea Harbour.

I am of Cork. I can keep a secret. I stopper for my own
bottled-up business,

took my personal oath of abjuration:

I abjure, renounce and abhor empire's supremacy and
    authority
over humanity in general and myself in particular.

I come from Cork of the mighty river Lee, of crystalline
    streams,
green mountains and hills.

I unable seaman brave the ocean; fortunate not to have been
    born
a woman.

For women overboard are drawn down to sea's floor;
weighted as they are by long reach-me-down drawers,
wool stockings thick as porridge, bone stays,
follow-behind-trains and bustles, iron-hoop crinolines,
petticoats, leg o'mutton-sleeved dresses,
weighty as the Queen's dusty old parlour drapery,
their family's saved-up gold guineas stitched into seams;
babes suckling at breasts, small barnacles clinging to hems.

For Lee Jenkins – Cork

Unlike those drowned Africans who are clad scant;
there's equal opportunity for watergrave available
to enslaved women and men,

ten times ten thousand sleep upon the floor of the sea,

but I'm of Cork.

My Aunt Rose was George O'Brian Wilson's favourite.
He'd give her six soda biscuits from a battered tin.
To the other grandchildren he'd dole out two biscuits each,
     saying:
'Life's not fair's the lesson here I'm trying to teach.'
On this one thing all agree: he religiously kept up
     St Patrick's Day.

Same time every year, him and him friend dem congregate
     and drink
and sing and jig.
Him and him wild friends dem who march down like a
     band of old soldier
from a place name Vinegar Hill.

Vineega. My mother and her people pronounced it, Vineega.
He and the remnant from Vinegar Hill drank and fiddled
     and jigged,
offering up high praises to their beloved Saint Patrick,

in that small village where Africans did not fail to venerate
in chant and drum-sound their own saints.
O the mix and mash up that went on in that place,
to the melodies of Europe
rolled the riddims of the Congo:

Redemption Ground

Bob Marley become the avatar.

For if in winter I fall asleep listening to Dolores Keane
I am guaranteed to be transported to the Island

where Jamaicans have a peculiar habit of calling all flowers
    roses.

Like the people of Hibernia we exalt the rose.
Unlike in other places, the Jamaican rose is ungendered.
There is even a posse of Jamaican macho men who call
    themselves,
'Black Roses'.

To us all flowers are roses
Accompong is Ashanti, root Nyomekopan
Appropriate name Accompong meaning warrior
or lone one. Accompong
home to bushmasters, bushmasters being
maroons, maroons dwell in deep places,
deep mountainous, sealed
strangers unwelcome, Mi no send you no come.

I love so the names of this place
how they spring brilliant like roses
to us all flowers are roses
engage you in flirtation, what is their meaning
pronunciation? A strong young breeze that just takes
these names like blossoms and waltz them around
turn and wheel them on the tongue.

There are angels in St Catherine somewhere.
Arawak is a post office in St Ann.

For Lee Jenkins – Cork

And if the Spaniards hear of this
will they come again in caravels
to a post office in suits of mail
to inquire after any remaining Arawaks.
Nice people, so gentle peaceful and hospitable.

There is everywhere here;
there is Alps and Lapland and Berlin
and there is, Carrickfergus, Clonmel, Donegal
Hibernia, Kildare, Newry, Middleton,
Waterford and Ulster Spring…

I walked to school down Leinster Road
in a city where Leitrim, Antrim, Killarney, Dublin,
Clare, Waterford, Armagh and Sligo were brought
from counties down to avenues and roads.

Honour to the Ones Transported.

Honour to the one who passed from the Nonesuch caves;
fossils of sea creatures shellacked to cave walls;

starfish medals pinned to cave-chests phosphorescent
beam-back to the ones lost on crossings.

Honour to those far from ground of where born;
who faced the sea with full heart and called
a new green field, Athenry.

For the ones force-shipped, as units of labour, for
        rebellion,
for stealing of Trevelyan's corn, the ones bonded
to sing praise songs in strange lands,

who stripped off names like shirts and shifts of cotton or flax;
and lay them down as place markers of homeland.

Ireland lived at our neighbours' the Lynches.

Mr Lynch, a man who could have walked undifferentiated
through any county of Ireland.

A man who named his son Dreamy; and his daughter
    Patsy.

A travelling salesman who belonged in the pages of
    Ulysses,
or on stage as a character in a play by Eugene O'Neill.
A man who'd done his wife some beyond-repair wrong
for she kept up spite and maliced him, till one day
she made her way across Busha Lynch's flat Bridge,
passed through Bog walk and went to live in Sligoville.
First free village for the unslaved; Sligoville where you
looked for William Butler Yeats.

Country Sligoville,
I will arise and go with William Butler Yeats
to country Sligoville
in the shamrock-green hills of St Catherine.

We walk and palaver by the Rio Cobre
till we hear tributaries join and sing
water songs of nixies.

Dark tales of maroon warriors
fierce women and men
bush comrades of Cuchulain.

For Lee Jenkins – Cork

We swap duppy stories, dark night doings.
I show him the link of a rolling calf's chain
and an old hige's skin carcass.

Love descended from thickets of stars
to light Yeats's late years with dreamings
alone. I record the mermaid's soft keenings.

William Butler I swear my dead mother
embraced me. I then washed off my heart
with the amniotic waters of a green coconut.

In December Sally water will go down
to the Sally gardens with her saucer
to rise and dry her weeping orbs,

O to live Innisfree in a hut of wattles and daub.

My mother's maternal grandfather would never visit
    Duanvale.
Duin means dark he said; and he himself had passed
through darkness. He had not part nor lot with David's
    psalms;
he had passed barefoot, bareback through the valley of the
    shadow.

He would never again be shoeless: he became a cobbler.
He would never again be bareback: he became a saddler.
He was a man of large appetites: he had known great
    hunger.
He had been a man comfortless: he took a creole wife,
he took my Guinea great grandmother.

Redemption Ground

And I lived for thirty years near the cooperage in
   St Andrew hills
where wild Irish boys once steam-bent wooden staves
into big-bellied barrels strong to contain sugar seas
of amber rum.

Rowdy, rowdy, rowdy all the way home.

Passing by Dublin Castle on the way to Irish Town
stopping in at Red Light to visit the soldier Pegeens;
comfort women, comforters of the regiment.

Others called them Soldier Peggy; Pegeen, Pegeen,
my mother said.

My Aunt Ann married a man name of Moran. A brown man
with eyes like peridots which happen to be my own
   birthstone.

Peridot: gemstone of ones born under the sign of the Lion.

The man had lion eyes.

My Aunt Ann was alright with being by blood and marriage
somewhat Irish. She showed love for the sons and daughters
of Kathleen O'Houlihan by hailing cabs for those who'd tied
   one too many on.
Many is the cab fare and steadying hand she gave to any
   Dicey Riley
taken to the sup upon St Paddy's Day on Montreal's streets.

And every year she'd order by catalogue, boots that seal
   snow and ice
from sole, crafted by Irish cobblers.

For Lee Jenkins – Cork

How do you feel about all this mix-up, this advantage-taking
white man taking advantage of African woman business.
Enraged? Angry? Bitter? Conflicted? All those things.

Hear Ann: No use eating out your liver over what done
happen already—
Have you seen what hate can do to a body?

How it can duin.

My aunts all went to sea themselves. Booked passage, boarded
vessels, crossed oceans, made their own luck in foreign lands
like O'Brian Wilson.

My aunt Ann loved the duin of her skin, dark as the cocoa
her own father cultivated. He, a man who wanted no part
of cane's history, preferred to sweeten his morning mug
of coffee or cocoa tea with logwood honey.
Reconciled with what occurred in that small village my
    Aunt Ann would say:
Our people, they came from all over. Some were sons of
bitches, some were good people, some were chancers, some
deserve honour, and at least one was a near-saint. They were
griots and storytellers, free and enslaved, they were pagans,
they were mystics, and did I mention a few were sons of
bitches? But all of them made us, she said, and all of them
made you a poet.

19

A party for Tarquin

So, THAT Saturday night I was staying home. Happily staying home. I didn't have a date, didn't have a boyfriend. I
didn't feel like hanging out with the girls or with my gay
fashion designer/dancer friend. I'd decided I was going to
go to bed early and read till I fell asleep; I'd probably listen
to conjure-man Miles Davis playing soft and low *Someday
My Prince Will Come* which was my go-to album when I
wanted to be alone.

But, just as I was about to slip into my nightgown, the
phone rang. It was Bernard asking, 'Hey, want to go to a party?'

'No, not really.'

'I bet you'll change your mind if I tell you it's a party for
Sir Laurence Olivier's son.'

'So how come you're invited?'

The minute I asked that, I knew there was a catch.

'Oh God, Bernard don't tell me this is another one of your
little social climbing moves.'

'No, man,' he whispers. 'It's Felicity.'

'So, you need me to protect you from her. Not doing it.'

'Actually, I told her you and I are a serious item, and I think she's determined to take me away from you.'

'Eff off.'

'Just come, do, please. It will be a nice lime' (which is what people from the Eastern Caribbean call what you do when you hang out and party with your friends) 'and you can meet Felicity.'

'Bernard, I'm not your dober-girl pinscher.'

And just as I was about to launch into a speech about friends not using friends I experienced a soft punch to my heart. Just like that, as if some hand rolled into a loose fist inside a soft suede glove had bopped me gently on the left side of my chest, and I thought, no, friends take stuff for friends. For family and for friends. That's what you do, that is just what we do.

My dear Bernard loved the idea of being able to say he'd been to a party where he met Sir Laurence Olivier's son. We, his friends, gave him hell about his predilection for social climbing, and he would just laugh and says something like, 'Do you know who I met yesterday? Peter Finch! His wife Eletha is a Jamaican, and they came to the hospital to see her mother.' Bernard was a sweet soul, all his friends loved him because he was kind, funny, handsome, brilliant and if it wasn't for his always wanting to hobnob with the nobs I guess he would have been perfect.

So, Felicity. She was a doctor at the hospital where Bernard was an intern and was determined to bed him. Felicity was no fool, she had sized my friend up, and identified his weak spot. An invitation to a party for Sir Laurence Olivier's son hosted by some other member of the island's British expatriate community would reel Bernard in, and she was so determined to get him that she even agreed that he could bring along his girlfriend (me).

So, I went along, and I won't wait till the end of this to say I'm glad I did because my friend died about ten years later and I'm grateful for every single memory I have of him.

I scrapped my plans to envelop myself in a cloud of baby powder, and ease into my white cotton nightgown, and instead I got dressed up in an outfit that, as I think about it, would be right in *Vogue* (literally) today. It was reddish and gold jersey and the top could be worn by itself as a mini dress or over the matching narrow-cut pants. I finished it off with a long narrow scarf loosely draped round my neck with one end flung carelessly over my left shoulder.

They arrived in Felicity's red sports car and I met said Felicity for the first time, she was from England and looked to be at least thirty.

'Oh God, girl, you look great,' gushed Bernard, clasping me to his bosom.

'Hello,' said Felicity. 'Nice to meet you, Bernard's told me so much about you.'

'And he's told me a lot about you.'

No, there was no time for a drink before heading out to the party, so we three packed into Felicity's red sports car. Felicity insisted that Bernard sat in the middle right next to her, and then I swear she said this:

'You won't know this, but there was a dancer named…'

'Isadora Duncan?' I said.

'Oh, you…'

'Yes, she was throttled by her scarf. It was blowing in the wind when she was driving a convertible and the scarf got hitched in the spokes of the car wheels.'

A party for Tarquin

People always assume that I don't know anything. I guess I just look as if I don't know anything. I have found that this can work in my favour; many is the time I have been greatly underestimated by people who have then written me off and left me alone to just get on with doing what I do.

Anyway, Felicity turned her red convertible down Hope Road and made a right turn when we got to the traffic light by Kings House and we took Lady Musgrave Road up to Barbican Road and we picked our way through Cherry Gardens in the cool November evening, the wind filling our hair as we breezed through Manor Park and began the ascent up Old Stony Hill Road. Felicity talked above the noise of the wind and the traffic, addressing all her comments in loud sideways volleys to Bernard, who was normally soft-spoken so only every second or third word or so of his could be heard above the noise of the traffic.

Felicity: 'SO...TARQUIN IS VISITING WITH SOME FRIENDS OF MINE – honkinghorns, whooshofwind, criesofvendors – WE ALL USED TO SHARE – honkinghorns, noiseofcarandtruckengines – A FLAT IN SLOANE SQUARE NEAR THE ROYAL COURT!'

Bernard: 'Oh, The ROYAL Court THEATRE! I SAW a very INTERESTING play there, I THINK it was called *SLAG*?'

Felicity: 'DID YOU REALLY? WHAT ARE THE ODDS! DAVID HARE IS A FRIEND! I WENT TO THE OPENING NIGHT... IT GOT PRETTY MIXED REVIEWS – honkinghorns, whooshofwind – I THOUGHT IT WAS A RIOT!'

Bernard: 'The staging was INTERESTING, especially that SCENE near the END at the tennis match blah blah blah blah...'

Honest to God. I spent some time in London once, and some friends and I used to go to the theatre. It so happens that one of the plays we saw was *Slag*. I hated it. I thought it was misogynistic, sexist and cruel. I found nothing in it to laugh about and I especially disliked that business of the false pregnancy. However, I was not going to say anything; that night I was only along for the ride as I waited for my prince to come.

While I was in London I also saw a musical called *Catch My Soul* based on *Othello*. Desdemona was played by the gorgeous African American singer and actress Marsha Hunt who went on to have a daughter with Mick Jagger.

I thought about Marsha Hunt right then as we drove along in that convertible because she had a splendid nimbus of an Afro which was exactly how I wore my own hair back then. I cannot imagine what my hair must have looked like after half an hour blowin' in the wind in Felicity's convertible.

Eventually we turned off Old Stony Hill Road and headed down a side road lined with pine trees. People who do not know Jamaica cannot imagine that there are places like that up in the hills just outside Kingston. The expatriate community has always preferred to live up in the hills where the temperature is invariably several degrees cooler than down on the plains. They take to the hills where they, or rather their gardeners, cultivate lovely gardens around their palatial houses.

Felicity eventually turned her red roadster into a driveway and proceeded to mount a really a steep hill that appeared to be as long as it was high.

I began to worry that her foot might slip and we'd plunge backwards down the slippery slope of the driveway and slide all the way down Stony Hill and end up back in Manor Park inside a coconut cart.

A party for Tarquin

But we reached the top eventually and there, set in a large lawn, was what looked like a sprawling great house that was in total darkness. 'Are you sure we have the right address?' Bernard whispered.

'Of course, love, I come here all the time.'

'It looks like everybody has gone to bed,' said I, as I jammed Bernard in the side with my elbow.

'No, no,' said Felicity. 'Maybe, ha, ha, maybe everyone just likes dancing in the dark.'

I opened my mouth to ask, 'Do you hear any music?' but I thought that remark might not help what was clearly an awkward situation. I decided to keep quiet, but I jammed my elbow into Bernard's side again, to say 'See what you've got me into?'

We got out of the car and Bernard and I followed Felicity as she marched up to the front door clutching a gift-wrapped bottle. She knocked. No answer.

She knocked again and called 'Helloooo! It's me, Felicity.'

The chirping of crickets was the only response.

I started to say, 'I think we should leave, don't you?'

Just then the front door opened less than halfway and a woman peeped round the door and said sleepily, 'Felicity?'

'Oh, hi, darling, we've come to the party.'

'You've come to the party? But, love, the party started this morning, and it ended hours ago.'

You had to give it to Felicity though; she stood firm, like the boy who stood on the burning deck, and holding her ground, declared, 'Well we're here, the party can start all over again.'

I swear the sleepy woman at the less-than-half-open-door muttered something that sounded like 'oh shit' then, 'I guess you might as well come in for a drink.'

At this point I was seriously thinking of saying to Bernard and Felicity, 'You two go ahead, I'll just stay in the car,' but I may have mentioned before that the entire place was in darkness, and who knew who or what was lurking in the Stony Hill bushes, ready to pounce upon a young woman (as I was then) sitting alone in a parked red convertible on the steep driveway of an expatriate couple.

The woman opened the door a little more and we filed in.

Felicity handed our reluctant hostess the bottle saying, 'Here, darling, I brought you some really good vino.'

The woman made her way into the kitchen and turned on one light.

That was it for lighting for the entire time we were there.

She did not invite us to sit down, but Felicity told us to take a seat, so Bernard and I made our way through the gloaming and sat in two chairs on either side of a big bay window. The sleepy woman then came out of the kitchen and handed us clear plastic glasses half-filled with tepid white wine.

Have you ever looked back and wondered about something you ate or drank? I found myself doing that after I read an interview with a famous chef who recommended that you should collect up all the dregs of wine left behind in glasses after a party, put it into plastic bags and freeze it for later use in sauces.

I know the domestic goddess said to use it in sauces, but what if somebody took that advice a step further and decided to just serve backwash wine to other unsuspecting guests? Anyway, after one sip of warm flat, I decided to let that cup pass.

I could feel Bernard refusing to look in my direction so for want of something better to do I studied the figure of a man, asleep on the couch, with his back to us. He appeared to be dressed all in white and what might have been a straw hat was set down on the floor in front of the sofa. He seemed to be sleeping very soundly and every now and again he made a whistling snuffly sort of sound, like babies make when they dream milky baby dreams. I could just make out that he was still wearing his shoes, and presumably his socks.

Meanwhile, at the long dining table at one end of the room, Felicity was engaging our reluctant hostess in lighthearted party chatter. 'So how was the party, then?'

'Oh, it was (yawn) fine.'

'Did Maxine and Donald come?'

'Yes, (yawn) they did.'

'How about Lucia? Did she and Graham manage to make it in from Ocho Rios?'

'Mmm, mmm.'

'So, tell me, how does Tarquin like being in Jamaica?'

'If he wakes up, he can tell you himself.'

'*Oh!* Is that him asleep over there? On the couch? Do you think he'd mind if I woke him, just to say hello? I didn't realise that that was him.'

'No, please don't wake him. I'm sure he would not take kindly to being woken up. He has to catch an early flight to Barbados tomorrow morning.'

'Oh, I was so hoping to catch up with him.'

This really is not going well, I thought. Any fool could see that very shortly our drowsy hostess would be showing us to the half-open door, and we would be wending our way back down Stony Hill. It looked like I would be spending the night listening to Miles after all.

Here's what I thought as we climbed back into Felicity's red car: Bernard can now tell everybody that he did meet

Sir Laurence Olivier's son and if he wants to make a joke of it he could say, 'I once met Sir Laurence Olivier's son and I could not wait to see the back of him,' which strictly speaking, would be true.

When we got to where I lived, I climbed out of the car threw a 'goodnight' over my shoulder and walked up the driveway to the front door.

Bernard was right behind me.

'Go away, you made me waste my whole evening. Why you making Felicity drive home by herself?'

'She'll be alright, I need a drink.'

He and I spent the rest of the evening laughing about the non-party; drinking an appalling bottle of wine, imported from, of all places, the vine (not vin) yards of Guyana. We also smoked an entire a pack of cigarettes between us while we listened to the Miles Davis sextet *Someday My Prince Will Come*.

That was the night I began to really appreciate the genius of the Jamaican-American pianist Wynton Kelly, about whom Miles himself was supposed to have said, 'Wynton is the light for the cigarette; without him there is no smoking.' That night I realised that if hope has a sound it would be Wynton Kelly's piano-playing. His hope notes were like sunbeams dancing on the morning waves coming in at Bluefields Beach.

And my friend just kept lifting the arm of the record player, over and over, he and I both, the two of us just kept playing the same track, 'Someday My Prince Will Come'.

20

Femme de la Martinique

FROM THE YOUNG girl in a beauty shop in a mall in Des Moines, Iowa, whose red mullet bristled like a fox's tail, who'd said, 'I just wouldn't like, have a clue like what to do with hair like yours,' to the older woman in the high street hairdressers in the north of England who looked as if she'd been hairdresser to the Brontë sisters, and who'd said, 'I niver dun air like yourn, lass,' the writer had become quite used to being told by hairdressers in different parts of the world that they did not do Black hair.

'There is a woman here who does hair like yours, but she's not working today.' That woman. She is perpetually on her day off from hair salons all over the western world. Why, just the day before the woman in this story had arrived in Paris she had tried to get her hair washed, calmed with conditioner, set on medium-sized rollers and dried under a hairdryer for half an hour, in a salon on London's Oxford Street, and she'd been told that the woman who did her kind of hair was not working that day. So, she'd arrived in Paris looking 'like a bush baby', as a hairdresser in Durban had once tactfully described her. But from the taxi on the way to her hotel she saw it, the answer to her hairdressing needs.

'Les Trois-Îlets' was lettered in gold leaf on the transom above the front door of the shop; and through the frosted glass of the French doors she'd been able to make out the figure of a dark-skinned woman. One day, she thought, I just might write a piece about trying to get my hair done in different places in the world, but really, she knew that she would never to do it. There is a list of topics that Black women writers often feel compelled to cover, Black women's hair being near the top of the list, but maybe there are enough people writing about that subject. Does the world really need another essay about Black women's hair?

The next day, after a breakfast of *café au lait* and a warm croissant she made her way from the hotel to Les Trois-Îlets. She had dressed carefully in a white silk blouse and a blue and white striped skirt. She'd hung the outfit on the hook behind the door of the tiny hotel bathroom so the steam from the shower would ease out the creases. This was a trick learned from a French-Canadian woman she'd once worked with whose name was Françoise, like Françoise Sagan, the author of *Bonjour tristesse*.

Bonjour Tristesse, Aimez-vous Brahms? and the stories of Colette had fed all her teenage fantasies about Paris. She had fallen in love with the idea of being in love in Paris and now, twenty-five years later, here she was, in Paris.

As she made her way from the hotel back to Les Trois-Îlets, she found herself humming Peter Sarstedt's song 'Where Do You Go To My Lovely' and after a while she realised that she was doing a kind of step and glide in time to the hurdy-gurdy waltz arrangement of the song. She quickly corrected her gait because she didn't want to look foolish.

What she wanted was to be taken for one of the fabulously dressed women looking all *soignées* and Parisian moving with such ease about the city. There were flower shops on almost every street corner. Buckets of springtime daffodils and peonies, lilies, jonquils, irises and roses scented the air, and perfectly dressed people sat at tables at pavement cafes and terraces flooded with sunlight. These smartly dressed shiny people all seemed to be drinking from gleaming goblets; everyone, everything in the city of light looked burnished, glowing.

As she made her way along the *rue*, she began to feel light-headed, as if she had sipped champagne mimosas for breakfast, but even in this faux mimosa state she could see clearly that the women she passed on the street all had hair that was well-coiffed and coloured, usually in intense shades of red or brown. All these Parisian women, even those in their nineties, looked perfectly turned out, groomed and smoothed, as if on their way to or from meeting a lover.

When she got to Les Trois-Îlets the door was locked and the dove-grey taffeta blinds folded down. She should have asked the clerk at the front desk to call. She began to worry that Les Trois-Îlets might be closed for the day. She decided to take a walk in the area and maybe do a little shopping.

She walked on to a shoe store a few shops down from the hairdressers. After looking at at least ten pairs of shoes, she went back to the very first pair she had tried on: wickedly expensive cobalt-blue suede sandals, but so elegant, so stylish, with subtle, classy little details, like small fringed tassels floating from the straps that wound twice around the ankles. When she stood before the mirror in the shoe store, she saw how they completed her navy blue and white ensemble, and she thought: when I get my hair done, I will be so pulled together. I will look like a woman Monet would have painted. I will feel perfectly put together when I stroll through the Luxembourg Gardens; I will cut a fine dash as I proceed in a leisurely way down the Boulevard Saint-Michel where Marie-Claire, the woman Peter Sarstedt sings about, lives in a fancy apartment with her collection of Rolling Stones records and someone who is friends with Sacha Distel.

The sandals came with a soft felt bag embroidered with a gold insect that could have been a bee. She peeled off quite a few traveller's cheques and paid for them, put her old shoes in the felt bag and walked back to Les Trois-Îlets, glancing down every few seconds to admire her own, now exquisitely shod, feet.

The dove-grey shades were up and the '*Fermé*' sign had been replaced by an '*Ouvert*' sign and when she pushed the door open, a bell rang and a tall, elegantly dressed woman *d'un certain âge* appeared from somewhere in the back of the shop.

'*Bonjour, mademoiselle, comment ça va?*'

'*Ça va bien. Parlez-vous anglais?*'

'*Oui.* Yes, I do.'

The elegant woman was from Martinique and her name was Hortense, and she used to be a fashion model. On the walls of the salon were many photographs of her on the covers of French fashion magazines, and a few images of her on the runway for top fashion designers, and a big blow up of her, and yes, Yves Saint Laurent, and she was wearing, without a blouse, one of his famous '*Le Smoking*' tuxedo suits, the lapels caught at the waist by a braided frog.

Hortense stood quietly, smiling and nodding as the writer inspected the photographs saying things like, 'These are all you, right?' and, 'Wow! Is this you and Yves Saint Laurent? Amazing!'

Finally, Hortense said: 'And 'ow can I 'elp you?'

Shaking her head from side to side, the writer ran one hand over her hair.

Hortense smiled. 'We need to fix that, *hein*? I have someone coming who has an appointment but if you can wait I will 'elp you, *d'accord*?'

A sleek car pulled up outside the salon, and a young woman who must have been at least six feet tall strode into Les Trois-Îlets. She was wearing jeans and a dark brown silk shirt; her hair was covered by a plaid silk scarf and most of her face was hidden by tortoiseshell-rimmed sunglasses.

She was carrying what the writer recognised (from reading high fashion magazines) as a Birkin bag: a handbag that cost as much as a significant down-payment on a one-bedroom apartment in many parts of the world.

There was much air-kissing and '*ma chérie*'-ing.

Then Hortense and the woman went into the area partitioned off from the main salon by a fall of grey curtains.

The writer sat happily, taking note of her surroundings. The walls of the salon were covered in grey water wave taffeta, and the chairs in the waiting area were upholstered in burgundy velvet which picked up the grey and burgundy tones in the carpet. In addition to the photographic display of Hortense in her glory days, there were several prints by Gauguin on the walls and a photograph of a small terracotta sculpture, captioned 'Femme de la Martinique'. The writer stared at the print of the small kneeling figure, which was dressed only in a *'foulard'*, the madras headwrap that was part of the national dress worn by women from Martinique. The statue's left arm was bent at the elbow and her hand inclined at the wrist was held upright between her breasts, as if in an attitude of devotion. This unusual feature made her look more like a figure on a Buddhist carving, which, the writer (a sometime painter and art critic) noted, made the small sculpture a cultural composite.

The writer remembered that Paul Gauguin had spent some time in Martinique, living in a lowly hut. The writer had once bought a refrigerator magnet depicting one of Gauguin's Martinique landscapes. Gorgeous. The pinkish clay of the unpaved path, the sable and green-blue rocks, the foam white flowers on a wayside bush, just a glimpse of cobalt-blue sea and not a living soul in evidence.

Hortense passed through the fall of sheer grey curtains.

'We can wash that hair now, *hein*?' Hortense washed and conditioned the writer's hair with products that smelt like khus khus grass, also known as vetiver, and jasmine. She explained that her products were all made exclusively for her clients, from ethically sourced organic products.

'The life of a model, it is *très dur* on the skin, on the hair, so much *maquillage*, so much heat. I know what it is like, I know, and so I opened this place, to help the Black models. My products, they are made in Martinique, they are *totalement naturels*.'

Gauguin's woman of Martinique looked out from the labels on the row of bottles on display above the wash basins; her left hand upraised as if to bless: blessed are the beautiful women who wash, cleanse and calm themselves with pure and fragrant soaps and unguents made by our lady Hortense.

Our lady Hortense then wrapped the writer's hair in a pale pink towel, told her to wait by the sink and disappeared again behind the curtain.

While the writer waited, she looked through the magazines on display on a gilded side table with cabriole legs. In an issue of *Vogue*, in a spread on the latest YSL collection, she recognised the model who had just come in, the one behind the curtain being tended to by Hortense. The model was hailed as the new Iman because she too was a student and was discovered by a famous American photographer while walking down the street of her East African home town.

The writer once read somewhere that fashion models are among the most insecure and neurotic people in the world. Here is why: they are routinely rejected, sometimes several times in a day, because no matter how beautiful you are, as a fashion model, you are not going to be selected for every single job. Maybe they need a brunette for the job, and you are a blonde. Maybe they need a young girl, and you are a model who has reached the ripe old age of, say, twenty-six. And so it goes.

Then Hortense reappeared with the model, whose face was covered with a treatment mask, which Hortense noted was made mostly from egg whites and lemon juice, to refine the pores. It made the skin on the model's face very taut and very shiny, as though she was swathed in cellophane. Her hair was now covered with a pearl-grey mushroom-shaped plastic cap and she was wearing a calf-length grey kimono. She looked very different from the vision toting the Birkin bag who strode into the salon half an hour earlier.

Hortense settled her under one of the two hairdryers set in an alcove at the back of the shop, then motioned to the writer to sit in the high chair facing the ornate mirror above her work station. She used her own brand of setting lotion and, when she squeezed some directly from the bottle onto the top of the writer's head, the Femme de la Martinique seemed to reach down from the label and lightly touch the writer on the crown of her head. Swiftly, deftly, Hortense parted her hair into sections then rolled it onto smooth plastic rollers. She tied a pink hairnet over the rollers and positioned the writer under the dryer next to the model.

The writer sat under the dryer and turned the pages of the latest *Vogue*, which happened to feature the model seated in the next chair, whose name, the writer learned from reading the captions accompanying her photographs, was Mathilde.

Mathilde walking the runway, Mathilde in an advertisement for perfume, Mathilde at a party, champagne flute in hand, head thrown back, eyes shut tight, wide and perfect mouth open as if to drink in all the flavours of the lovely It-girl life.

And the writer was sitting beside her, in Paris no less! She shifted her head slightly inside the dryer in order to glance at the real Mathilde, as she studied the images of Mathilde caught on the page. Nobody is going to believe this, she thought. I best just keep this one to myself, people already believe that because I'm a writer I exaggerate, and I sometimes do, but this time they'll accuse me of showing off if I tell them that I managed to find myself sitting in a salon in Paris, next to a famous model, who in person looks much darker than she does in all her pictures. A famous model who at this moment looked nothing like the picture of the fabulous bird of paradise streaming down the runway in an elaborate hand-embroidered ballgown.

Suddenly the model pushed the metal cone of the hairdryer back and turned to the writer. She smiled and said 'I must tell you, your sandals? *Très jolies!*'

The writer pushed back her dryer too, she was so pleased that the model liked her sandals. '*Merci beaucoup*... Thank you.' And, pointing to the model's face on the cover of *Vogue*, the writer said, 'And congratulations to you. This is so, so wonderful!'

'You are good to recognise me looking like this!'

And they both laughed.

Maybe, after that laugh, the writer should have just stopped.

She should have just felt pleased that the famous model had been nice enough to compliment her on her exquisite taste in footwear.

She should have just felt happy that her choice of sandals had received the seal of approval from one of the world's top fashion models, but no, she had to go on and say something more, just had to say one more thing, something she imagined the model would have liked to hear. She said, 'Your family must be so proud and happy.'

But when she said that the model said nothing.

There was an awkward silence before the model pointed to her own face on the cover of the magazine and said, '*Ma famille*? *Non*. Proud? *Non*. My father? He does not like these photographs. He will have no pictures of me in his house. He told me, "I do not know you." He says I have turned myself into a ghost. My brothers? They are crazy, crazy. They say I sell my body. One of them, he tells anyone who asks about me that I am a prostitute in Paris. *Non, ma chère*, they are not proud of me, they are happy to take the money I send, yes, but proud of me? *Non*.'

The famous fashion model looked so sad, so distraught under the patina of her egg-white and lemon mask that the writer was tempted to get up from under the hairdryer and give her a big hug, but she thought that might seem overly familiar. Instead she murmured that she was sorry, so sorry to hear that. Then they both put their heads back up inside the metal cones and sat staring out at the blurred stream of traffic through the frosted glass doors of Les Trois-Îlets.

But when the writer's hair was dry, and Hortense had brushed and styled it so her face was framed by big loose curls, and after she'd paid her, and said *merci beaucoup*, and *au revoir* with a softening of the 're' so it sounded like 'au voir', and after she'd waved goodbye to Mathilde who was having her natural hair plaited into cornrows so that Hortense could sew onto them, with a big-eyed bone needle, long falls of blue-black human hair imported from India, the writer stepped out into the spring sunshine and turned her face in the direction of the Boulevard Saint-Michel. I am now well put together, she thought to herself. I am now well put together upon this gorgeous day in spring. In Paris!

YEARS LATER, the writer is sitting up in bed in a hotel room in New York. Walking about the streets earlier that day she'd noticed the many young Black New Yorkers sporting extravagant natural hairdos. She wonders to herself just how many hairdressers have been put out of business by these fine and confident young Black women who look as if they roll out of bed, shower, dress, and then just shake their heads vigorously from side to side. Wild and woolly tresses taken care of. Hairstyle that. Love it.

Femme de la Martinique

She turns on the television set and sees scenes of carnage in Paris. Parisians out dining, some attending a rock concert, others cheering on their team at a soccer game in a stadium, blown-up, murdered and maimed by hate-crazed zealots who condemn the city of light as the city of prostitution and decadence. And she remembers Hortense and Les Trois-Îlets and Mathilde whose brothers take her money even as they accuse her of selling herself, and who are crazy! Crazy!

21

The waterman

OFF-WHITE PLATES *were prized by the ancient Chinese because they reminded them of the moon.* She placed her knife and fork at the twelve o'clock position on her plate and sat back in her chair; then she immediately leaned forward and with her right forefinger shifted the tines of the fork so the cutlery hands on the china plate clock face read more like eleven than twelve o'clock. As she got up from the table she remembered that the sentence about off-white plates and the moon came from one of her textbooks on pottery-making.

'Excuse me... the baby...'

'You are excused,' the hostess said.

As she left the table the hostess began to tell a joke that she had heard many times before.

She wanted to get home before the clock struck midnight. She made her way from the dining room through the living room, down a long passage to the family room where the children of the house were watching TV.

The waterman

Her son was half-asleep on one of the sofas with a fort of cushions set up around him to prevent him from falling onto the floor.

'Come on, baby, we're going home,' she said to the drowsy one-year-old in his yellow flannel one-piece pyjamas. She pressed her face into the flannel belly of the sleepy bundle and inhaled his delicious smell of milk spit-up, Woodwards gripe water, baby powder, pee, and clean baby. She almost burst into tears, so in love was she. Stepping in the spaces between the children sprawled out on the carpet she sang 'Happy New Year to you, Happy New Year to you, Happy New Year to you.'

'Happy New Year, Auntie,' chorused the children of the house, never taking their eyes off the television screen where a cartoon Bob Cratchit was hoisting a cartoon Tiny Tim up unto his shoulders, so the sweet-faced boy could pipe in dulcet tones, 'God bless us, everyone.' This Christmas classic courtesy of Disney.

Not inclined to give any excuses as to why she was leaving before midnight, she bypassed the dining room by exiting through the kitchen, which had a side door that led out to the yard where her car was parked.

One of the hostess's pointed remarks disguised as a joke made earlier in the evening had been about how 'eccentric' she was since she had become a mother. If she had thought of it then, she could have made a witty comeback by quoting something from Bertrand Russell about not being afraid of being regarded as eccentric. But that evening she could not remember any quotation from anybody because she suffered a lot from a condition that could be called foggy baby brain, baby on the brain, all her mental resources marshalled to cope with taking care of teething baby, colicky baby, restless baby, don't-know-why-baby-is-crying-baby.

If that blue-skinned genie in one of those Disney movies could materialise and grant her three wishes, one of those wishes would be a week's sleep.

She'd just sat at the dinner table and smiled and shrugged when her hostess had dropped the charge of eccentricity on her. She'd thought to herself, I'd rather plunge my arms up to the elbows in a bucket of poop-filled nappies than expend any effort defending myself against charges of eccentricity from this woman who is waiting for me to return to being the aimless single woman, always available to her friends, that I used to be before the advent of baby.

Not one more New Year's Eve like this. Not one more New Year's Eve pretending she was having a good time.

She lay the baby down in his wicker bassinet in the back seat of her car and tucked him in tight with his blue blanket appliqued all over with gambolling satin sheep. The car was small and rode close to the ground and the hum of the engine soon lulled the baby to sleep. She turned into her driveway at 11.20. She put the baby to bed and midnight found her raising a solitary toast to the new year with a cup of mint tea.

In the morning she got up and went to the bathroom and turned on the tap to find there was no water. There are over one hundred rivers on the island of Jamaica. 'Xamayca' is supposed to mean Land of Wood and Water; water, water everywhere, and not a drop to drink, bathe in, cook with or flush your toilet! Here it was, the first day of a brand-new year and she had no water to wash herself, to bathe the baby, to flush the toilet. O shit!

The woman who took care of her son for her on weekdays, when she went out to work, had told her about the waterman. It seemed this man, by virtue of being put in charge of turning on and off the valves of the communal water tank, had become, almost overnight, the most powerful person in their small hilltop village.

She herself had never actually seen the waterman, but there were stories circulating in the village that, if you angered the waterman he would make sure that no water ran through the pipes to your house. They also said that if you bribed him, the waterman would make sure that your pipes never ran dry.

After a while the waterman began to assume mythic status; it was as if he was some Arawak god who had to be placated by having his name called over and over by the awestruck people of the village.

So, this morning, she woke to find that she had been caught unprepared – *I mean seriously, who would expect the water to be locked off on New Year's Day?* – and that she had forgotten to fill the large plastic bottles that had become a fixture in most Jamaican kitchens, and that she had neglected to fill the bathtub the night before with enough water to bathe in and flush the toilet. She thought, I have no choice, I have to go in search of the goddamn waterman, to see if I can persuade him to turn on the water.

So, after making herself a cup of tea and fixing the baby's morning cereal with water from one of the two bottles in the refrigerator, boiled in a pot on top of the stove, she fed the baby, wiped his round brown limbs down with a rag dampened with the rest of the warm water and then used the same rag to wipe her face. She dressed the baby, then dressed herself, feeling a little out of sorts and irritable because she really needed a shower.

She had no idea where to find the waterman, so she drove to the house of the woman who looked after her son when she went out to work. When she got there, the front door of the small wooden house was locked, and the jalousie windows shut. Only a yapping mawga dog ran out to the gate when she drove up; she honked the horn a few times and called out, 'Good morning, anybody at home?' but no one answered. She remembered that her son's babysitter had a new boyfriend who lived in town. They must have gone to a dance on New Year's Eve and stayed over at his place. That was way more action than she herself saw last night.

She decided to drive down to the town square and see if anybody there knew the whereabouts of the waterman. To get to the square, she had to drive past the house of one of her friends.

She hoped she wouldn't see her erstwhile friend because she had stopped returning her calls. If she did see her, she would feel compelled to stop and have a pointless conversation with her for Auld Lang Syne, about things and people that no longer interested her, during which she was bound to feel at a disadvantage because she hadn't had a shower and her car really needed washing. God, what a way to start a new year! As she approached her friend's house she saw that there were cars parked outside and she could hear Home T-4 carolling 'Mek the Christmas Catch You in a Good Mood', one of her favourite Jamaican Christmas songs.

A passing glance at the laughing group on the wide verandah let her know that these were revellers who had partied in the New Year and were now keeping the revelry going at a bang-up New Year's Day breakfast/brunch.

As she shifted into third gear, sped up and drove determinedly past the house, she wondered if she was just jealous of her friends. After all, they were bringing in the New Year in style and here she was, a sad figure searching for the waterman on New Year's Day. Perhaps she was somewhat jealous, but she was also quite certain that she didn't want to be back there on the verandah with her old friends because she'd done enough of that. There was no doubt in her mind that that particular phase of her life had ended, but she had no idea what form the next one would take.

Your life is supposed to go somewhere. You are supposed to start somewhere and end up somewhere, preferably in a better place than the one where you started.

One Easter Sunday when she was twelve years old, the sight of the bell-mouthed lilies on the altar dripping with ice-white lace cloths, the tall white candles burning in the brass candleholders and the smoke and scent of incense streaming from the brass thurible swung from the end of a long brass chain had propelled her up and out of herself, and for the entire service she had hovered somewhere between her pew and the vaulted church ceiling in a state of pure bliss. She remembers thinking to herself that, if she'd died then, she would surely have been taken up into heaven.

There was no sign of anybody who could be the waterman in the town square, which looked, on New Year's Day, like the deserted streets of a town in a cowboy movie.

There was absolutely no point in asking the one drunken man – who presumably had no family, or else why would he be leaning cross-legged like Lee Marvin's horse in the movie *Cat Ballou*, against the door frame of the village rum bar on the morning of New Year's Day? The drunken man was calling out to everyone who passed by, 'Happynewyear! Happynewyear!'

Maybe he was, despite all appearances, really happy. It occurred to her right then that the drunk was what Jamaicans would refer to as: 'a waters man' and she was looking for 'the waterman.' And that stupid lame joke made her laugh, and after she had laughed she felt a little more like herself.

She turned the car around and headed back home. She fed the baby tepid orange juice from a sippy cup and gave him two arrowroot biscuits which he gummed away at, one in each fist, like a sweet old man. She changed his diaper and put him in his play pen, where he promptly fell asleep with the biscuits mushing in his chubby fists.

She then had an idea. If she melted the ice cubes from the freezer, she'd get nice cold ice water. She opened the refrigerator to find that the ice cubes had started melting without her. Stale and flat, that was how that water would taste. Power cut. No light, no water. Happynewyear to you too.

She needed to wash the baby's clothes. She needed to wash herself.

She needed to wash herself of what was beginning to feel like a fine dusting of sand and salt that had sifted down over her and her whole life, over her dreams of finding true love and interesting rewarding work, and good friends. She really wished she had all those things but mostly she needed access to water: cool clear water. She began to hum that song that she'd read somewhere was about a man hallucinating about finding water as he crossed the desert.

I'll do a rain dance, she thought. I will not just hum, I will do a rain dance.

I'll make my limbs rise and fall down like rain. I will face the Blue Mountains, which was surely what the Tainos – who she had been taught were called Arawaks – did when they prayed for rain.

So, taking off her sandals, she stepped out onto the wooden verandah and she faced the mountain and proceeded

138

to dance while the baby slept there in the living room in his play pen.

She whirled round and round as she danced, she hummed as she danced, then she danced jumping up and down Rastafari Nyabinghi style, hopping from one foot to the other, then lunging forward, harder and harder until she realised that she might wake the baby, and with no water to wash him it was best that he slept a while longer.

She sat down cross-legged on the verandah and attempted to visualise sheets of rain dropping down from the sky, a technique she had learned when she once did some classes in Transcendental Meditation.

It had been drizzling the second time she saw him. The truth was she had been walking by his house on purpose; and there he was in the driveway, putting up the top on his sports car. He had not seemed surprised to see her; he just said, 'Come inside or you'll get really wet. I'm about to have lunch, you can have half my sandwich.' She remembered that once they went inside the sun came out, and it did not rain.

Just like that. If she'd believed then in action at a distance, and using mental powers to draw people to you she would have sworn some force like that was at work pulling her to him. He was at least ten years older than her, he was a somebody. She was eighteen years old. She'd met him at a birthday party given by one of her friends the week before. He lived around the corner from her friend, who'd asked him because he was a somebody, to come to the party as the master of ceremonies.

She'd been standing over by a window, and after he'd finished his MC spiel he'd walked straight over to her and said something quite ordinary, something like, 'God, it's hot

in here, I'm going to stand by this window right beside you.'
And she'd fallen in love for the first time, just so.

She had felt as if she were bathing in warm water all the
time she was with him. He'd taken her out to see a play, and
they'd met for lunch two or three times and they'd spent the
afternoon together the day before he left the island. They'd
talked a lot, about music, about books, about movies; he
used words like unexpurgated and bowdlerised when they
discussed books, and he'd given her some of his books
because he was heading off to England to study law. On their
last afternoon together he'd said, 'I so want to be the first
man to make love to you, but I need time, way more time
than I have now.' So he concentrated on doing two things:
he gently probed the outer corner of her mouth with the tip
of his tongue until he set off starbursts in her brain, and he
stroked her body slowly so that she'd risen up out of herself
and hovered between the floor and the ceiling just like that
time she'd had the transcendent experience in church. As
a farewell present he gave her his collection of books by
Bertrand Russell, a copy of sayings by Nietzsche and a well-
thumbed copy of *Atlas Shrugged* by Ayn Rand.

After he left she bought a copy of Dionne Warwick
singing 'Trains and Boats and Planes' and played it and
played it as she wept. She also stopped going to church.

The baby woke up cooing and smiling like a small jovial
Buddha. He wanted to play, kicking his chubby arms and
legs and blowing spit bubbles. She loved him so, she loved
him so, she loved him so much. She loved him so much she
knew that if she had to, she would die for him.

Later that day she paid a small boy who was walking by
her house to draw water from the river that ran through the
village. Sediment settled in the bottom of the plastic bottles

as the river was running low, and she used the grey water to flush the toilet.

And that night she made sure to stay up until after midnight when the waterman magnanimously turned the water back on for four hours, and she filled every container in the house with water, and she had a long shower and washed her hair at 1am on January 2nd. Later that day, she went through her bookcase till she found all the books he had gifted her. On the flyleaf of each collection he had written something cryptic and koan-like in his bold hand, and he'd signed with his initials. She remembers he'd used a fountain pen. She remembers that she'd read 'Why I am Not a Christian', and that she'd tried hard to agree with what Bertrand Russell wrote, but somehow she could never fully get his point of view, and she'd stopped reading that book because, she'd told herself, she wasn't bright enough to understand it. She'd felt the same way when she tried to agree with Nietzsche that God was dead.

She leafed through the books and noted that he had underlined passage after passage; she finally settled on one from Bertrand Russell's *The Conquest of Happiness*: 'You can get away from envy by enjoying the pleasures that come your way, by doing the work you have to do, and by avoiding comparisons with those you imagine, perhaps quite falsely, to be more fortunate than yourself.'

And that would always make great sense to her.

She'd been only eighteen years old, and she had read those books he'd gifted her as if they were holy texts, concentrating really hard to absorb the ideas generated from the mind of an upper-class Englishman, and a hardcore Übermensch. She concluded that some of what they wrote contained great wisdom, but not much of it had ever really been useful to her. Then she thumbed through the copy of *Atlas Shrugged* and wondered why she'd spent so much time trying to relate to the words of a control-freak of a woman with ice in her veins, a woman who was all about WILL, and being harder than the rest. Arrrgh! She had spent countless hours bending her mind to agree to their take on life.

The time had come to really search for spiritual nourishment. She needed to read living words that would nourish her so she could nourish the baby; maybe she'd even have to write them herself. She packed the books in a cardboard box. When she moved from that house she'd leave them behind.

What she needed now, cool clear water. She needed it now more than ever, not just for herself, but for the life she had brought into the world. The world, which, when the baby boy smiled and warbled and babbled sweet baby glossolalia, was the exact opposite of horrible. The father of the baby liked poetry. They once wrote a play together. He was writing a novel, a coming-of-age story. They were trying to make it work. The world was not horrible, horrible, horrible as one of those books claimed.

Years later, when she met the man who would become her husband, his first present to her was a Waterman fountain pen.

22

Parliament Street

'They've really fixed up that Tim Horton's nicely,
haven't they?'
'Yes, and we, the people of Parliament Street, will
soon fix that.
I tell you this street is really changing.'

I OVERHEARD this conversation outside one of those spiffy coffee-shop-slash-pubs on Parliament Street. The guy who said the street was changing was talking to a man who looked just like that actor who stars in *Da Vinci's Inquest*.

I wouldn't know, I'm fairly new around here, but the *Da Vinci's Inquest* guy, who looks just as handsome in real life as he does on TV (if it was in fact him), seemed a little cast down to hear the news that Parliament Street was changing.

I don't know what it used to be like, but here's what I like about it now: on some days it looks like I imagine the Kingdom of Heaven is supposed to look, with every conceivable type of person walking up and down going about their business. Actually some, like the group in their wheelchairs who congregate at the corner of Amelia and Parliament, are not, strictly speaking, walking up and down, but there they are. And the very posh people who patronise the fine French restaurant along Amelia Street have to make their way past the social club of the motorised wheelchair people, who are definitely not posh.

I'm not sure how she will fit into my Kingdom of Heaven analogy, except maybe as a reincarnation of Rahab the harlot gone back to her old ways, but there is this one girl who openly propositions men at the intersections along Parliament Street in broad daylight. A tall, rangy girl who has that model's springbok walk. She is sometimes dressed in an expensive-looking leather jacket, and she probably used to be very beautiful, but now her face looks like too much life on the streets has rearranged her features so that when you look at her you look quickly away. I once heard a taxi driver threaten to run her over with his cab after she stuck her head in his window and said something to him.

Today I had lunch with my friend Isabel. She is a very important lady in this town, but unlike a lot of people who consider themselves to be really important she is one of the warmest and most generous-hearted people I have ever met, and lunch with her always strengthens my faith in humanity.

After lunch with Isabel, I decide to take a walk. It's an early fall day, a Kingdom of Heaven kind of day, because the people you pass on the street all look burnished and smiling, like they've eaten their fill of inky sweet blueberries and golden Ontario corn.

I cherish what I think of as my silent times. Times when I spend at least six or seven hours by myself, not speaking even one word out loud. I'm a big fan of Thomas Merton, who was a Trappist monk, but even before I started to read his books I liked the idea of being silent for set periods of time. After those self-imposed silences I tend to talk too much in big over-excited bursts.

I get to the corner of Parliament and Dundas and I turn right. Maybe I'll just walk down to the Eaton Centre and get myself a new sweater for winter is a comin', sure as fate. Dundas is a strange street. There are whole blocks that seem almost abandoned, lonely, scary, even at three o'clock in the afternoon.

And then I see them up ahead. The two women.

When I get closer I notice that one is older. The younger one is maybe twenty years old. They are both shading their eyes. The older one is saying something about how they should eat now before things get really busy later.

The younger, taller, dark-skinned one says something in a foreign language and then shakes her head, looks down at the pavement, holds both palms up to the sun and mutters 'Okay, okay.' She is dressed in a wide, gorgeous boubou, all deep blue and white. She looks like she is standing neck deep in the Atlantic Ocean and the swirls in the tie-dye pattern of her voluminous gown are frothy whitecaps of waves. The neckline dips in a style that I know, from being the daughter of a dressmaker, is called a boat neck. It slips and slides to one side to reveal a polished shoulder blade. She could easily have been posing for a spread in a fashion magazine right there on semi-deserted Dundas Street.

Then she looks up, drops her hands to her sides and sees me staring at her. She stares hard back at me and rolls her eyes back in her head. All you can see are the whites of her eyes. Jesus! I hurry past.

The older one looks as if she has a lily on her brow and anguish moist and fever dew. The faded rose on her cheek is fast withering too. The woman looks, like John Keats's knight at arms, as if 'La Belle Dame sans Merci', has her in thrall.

But the younger one, the Senegalese lady, she looks like really beautiful women in their twenties do, invincible, as if nothing, no power on earth will ever vanquish her. She looks as if she is certain she will never look as beaten down as her companion, the veteran of the flesh wars who is advising her to eat now before the fleet comes in for servicing, before the raft of Johns rolls in. Maybe feral lady is fresh off the boat herself and is working to pay back her passage. Maybe she is a victim of human trafficking.

It could well be, you know. It's likely that she has a pimp who has put her to work in this run-down place.

This is very depressing.

I ONCE KNEW a girl who used to be a prostitute. By the time I met her she had left that life behind and was working as what was then called an 'office maid', serving tea and coffee and taking the mail to the post office and things like that, at a place where I used to work.

When she brought round the tea and coffee at ten o'clock, she would make sure that she brought me my tea last. At first, I was puzzled about this, and then I realised that when she brought me my tea she would always stay to talk with me about something. She'd hold the metal tea tray up before her chest like a shield, and she'd say something like, 'The tea taste alright?'

And I'd say, 'Yes thanks.'

Then she'd ask to borrow a magazine, saying, 'I will bring it back tomorrow.'

I started bringing her books and magazines from home, and one day I showed her a short story of mine that had been published in the Sunday paper.

The next day, when she brought my tea, she said: 'Suppose I tell you that I could write a book about my life.'

And before I could tell her that everybody I know thinks that their life story is interesting enough to become a book, she said, 'Tell me if you think this don't belong in a book…'

'Is a whole heap a children my mother have, and because I was bright in school, she send mi to Kingston to live with this lady who say she was looking for a schoolgirl to do little things around the house for her and her family and that she would take care of mi and send mi to school.

'The lady and her husband have a rum bar and a club, and one day she tell mi that I was to start help out in the rum bar. I never did too like it, but I never know what else to do. And little by little them just call on mi to "help out" more and more until she and him put mi to work in the club and that was, as my grandfather would say, the beginning of sorrows.

'Is just so I start to live bad life, a life I never want, but the lady husband threaten mi and say how mi ungrateful because is him and him wife put clothes on mi back and give mi food to eat, so mi owe them, and I better pay them and help out a situation. The lady, she say she was a Christian, say she personally would make sure I don't have to sell myself to any and everybody; so she always send some of the more decent-looking man to mi. This one man, him was older than my father, him start to come regular. Him always ask mi how mi feeling, and sometime him would bring a little present or so for mi. I did think him was such a decent man.

'Then one Sunday evening, I will never forget it, him come dress up in a good suit, but him wasn't looking all that well, and when I look in him face, my blood just run cold. I ask him, "You sure you alright?"

'And him say yes, and all him need was for me and him to go to bed.

'Well the next thing you know I hear him cry out loud loud and then I feel this heavy, heavy weight…'

She started crying uncontrollably when she came to this part of the story.

From what I could make out between her sobs, that terrible cry emitted by the man was not the sound of *la petite mort*, the man was dead.

There was an envelope addressed to her in his suit pocket. In the envelope was a note which thanked her for fulfilling his dream. His dream you see, had always been to die while having sex. To put it crudely, to come and go.

Maybe he had confided his ambition to his wife of many years, maybe she told him to never, ever touch her again which is why he ended up having his dream come true in a brothel where he decided to bestow on this young girl the honour of having him die inside her.

I TOLD HER to wait in my office, and I went to the staff kitchen and made her a cup of tea. I brought it back and she thanked me and drank it as we both sat in silence. My office was on the fifth floor and it had a window with a view of Kingston Harbour. I'm not sure that detail is important, but I remember looking out through the window at the Caribbean

Sea in the distance as we sat there in the aftermath of that terrible revelation.

'THE ONLY THING that save my life,' she said after a while, 'is that I read Psalms; every day, every night, I would be in the grave now if I never read Psalms.'

She said she ended up working in another nightclub/brothel.

Her saving grace was that no matter what was happening in her life she was always reading. She said she read a lot of *Reader's Digest*.

You ever notice how, no matter where you go, there always seems to be a copy of *Reader's Digest*? I don't know, there must be some secret society of people who go out in the dead of night, to distribute old copies of *Reader's Digest*.

Anyway, this poor girl said that a man who was a teacher and who was also a regular visitor to the nightclub, took notice of the fact that she was always reading, and struck up a friendship with her. He began to bring her books and he helped her to attend classes and to sit some GCE subjects which she passed, and that is how one day she was eventually able to leave that life behind her.

Now every time I read an article about prostitution or human sex-trafficking I think about this story and I think of those two women on Dundas. I wonder if they are still comrades in arms? Is the worn-out 'La Belle Dame sans Merci' one still standing? Does the beauty from Africa still stare hard and snarl at anybody who dares to look openly at her and wonder what's-a-nice-girl-like-you? I wonder if there will ever be a Time's Up or a Me Too movement for women like them.

23

Racism

THE TAXI DRIVER looked like one of those men I'd grown up seeing in photographs in the weekly edition of the *Daily Mirror*. An ordinary-looking middle-aged man, maybe in a feature about a punter who had won the pools and had been seen in his local pub buying pints for his mates.

I was totally taken aback when, as I gathered up my raincoat and bag to leave the taxi, he said to me, 'Go on back to the jungle, we don't want your kind over 'ere.' Cold as you please.

This was my first visit to England, 'the Motherland', and I'd been having a grand time up till that point.

I was, to say the least, shocked. And then something happened that I've never been able to explain. Right after he said those words I said, 'Thank you. Thank you very much for being so kind. You are the nicest, most polite person I have met since I've been here.'

I do not know how or why I responded in that way, but I realised immediately that those words had a strange effect on the driver, for he just stared blankly back at me and said nothing.

I got out of his vehicle and walked away, then turned and looked back to see the cab still parked in the same spot.

Knowingly or not, he'd dropped me off at the wrong address, and as I walked to my destination I kept looking back and seeing that the cab was still parked there at the exact spot where he'd dropped me off.

This was not the first time in my life I'd been at the receiving end of open racial abuse. Growing up in Jamaica I was always fully aware that Jamaicans practise their own shameful terrible forms of colour prejudice and that darker skinned Jamaicans were often considered less-than in a culture where people would say things like 'anything too black never good,' about their own selves.

But give thanks and praises to Marcus Garvey and to Rastafarians, who insisted that Black is Beautiful so there was something of a built-in corrective to that bullshit self-hating thinking that many Jamaicans wrestle with. That terrible self-hatred that manifests itself nowadays in skin-bleaching. Still, I insist there have always been Jamaicans who are very proud of their dark skin. 'Mi black but mi comely, a so di Queen a Sheba tell king Salaman, and me black and me well comely,' I once heard a woman on a street in Kingston say.

But back to where we left the London taxi driver.

To this day, I do not know why I said those words, instead of cursing back at him, which anybody who knows me knows that I am well capable of doing. In fact, that incident seemed to open the way for two other similar incidents (these tests always seem to come in threes) that I responded to in entirely different ways.

A few days after the taxi incident, I went, with two Jamaican friends (one whose name is Canute, yes, like the king who tried to stay the waves) to the theatre to see *Catch My Soul*, a musical inspired by Shakespeare's *Othello*. At the intermission, I went to the ladies' room, and while I was in there I heard the woman who was in charge of cleaning the bathrooms say to someone waiting outside the door, 'There's a nigger in there.'

When I came out, I said 'I heard you'; and then I said something I am now ashamed of, I said, 'What can I expect? You clean toilets.' Even then, I knew that there were perfectly decent people who clean toilets, but she was not one of them.

The next incident had to do with an advertising campaign for Australia. I had been assigned to a creative team at McCann who were working on a campaign for the Australian Tourist Board. I was happily contributing my opinions on copy and layout for the ads but when the day of the presentation came around I noticed everyone behaving awkwardly. The copywriter, whose name I do not remember, who was a light-skinned Indian woman, took me to one side and said 'Look, neither you nor I will be going into the presentation, because Australia has a "Whites Only" policy.' And there and then I remembered a sentence in one of my reading books at primary school that said – I swear it was written down there for us to read – 'Australia is a white man's country.' I responded to that incident by taking off early and walking around Kensington Market and deciding that I would never visit Australia. I still have not done so, but maybe I'm changing my mind about that. Especially after having spent so many years of my life living and working in the USA and Canada where I have grown used to random acts of racism: like the drunk in New York who spat at me in the street (luckily, he missed) and called me the N word. If you want to know what the temperature in the Arctic feels like, try being the only Black person in a room in some places in Canada.

But I still have to say that I was genuinely shocked that there were so many people in the state of Michigan, where I lived and worked for over twenty years – surely I met some of them – who voted for the 45th president and who still support him even after he failed to condemn tiki-torch bearing, hate-spewing neo-Nazis, and after what he said about immigration from Haiti and Africa and places where Black people come from.

I recently saw a brilliant documentary on James Baldwin, whose acuity of voice and vision is even more relevant today than before.

I am haunted by the story of Sandra Bland, who gets pulled over by a policeman who claimed she switched lanes without indicating, and who days later ended up hanging in a jail cell. All that I could do was write a poem.

'Say Her Name: Sandra Bland'

*O Sandra Bland she was cast in a low budget
remake of mean streets; as lone woman driver
who sights a cop car framed in her rearview mirror;
and in panic crosses the white line.*

*Blue uniform in a rage swears she did not indicate.
Fires orders for her to put out her cigarette.
She went off script; told him it was her car.
She was entitled to smoke in it if she wanted.*

The camera captures how she is flung to the curb.
Restrained then locked down in a jail cell
on the third day she rises hanged by the neck;
feet frantic pressing at the last on air brakes.

A critic on Fox writes her off; gives her a thumbs
. down for acting arrogant, not taking directions.
For her part all she did was leave home, drive
and change lanes. Say her name: Sandra Bland.

There are days when I admit to being genuinely afraid when I watch the news.

Maybe it is alright for me to go to Australia now.

Racists are everywhere. Jesus help us.

But fortunately, so are beautiful, righteous, decent, generous and loving people and I am lucky to call many such people friends and colleagues. Gracious, warm-hearted, loving, upright, caring human beings who live in Britain and in every state of the USA and all over Canada and just about everywhere I have ever been, and whom I am sure, greatly, thankfully, outnumber the vicious crazies with their tiki-torches and their hate and spite spit and worse, way worse, their guns and ammunition.

These are scary times. God help us.

24

For Keith Jarrett Rainmaker – Iowa City

Piano man,
my roots are African.
I dwell in the centre of the sun.
I am used to its warmth
I am used to its heat
I am seared by its vengeance,
(it has a vengeful streak)
my prayers are usually
for rain.

My people are farmers
and artists
sometimes the lines blur
and a painting becomes
a December of sorrel;
a carving heaps like a yam hill,
or a song of redemption

wings like petals
of resurrection lilies.

All these require rain.
So this Sunday
when my walk misses
my son's balance
on my hips,
I'll be alright
if you pull down
for me, waterfalls of rain.

I never thought a piano
could divine,
but I'm hearing you this morning
and right on time
its drizzling now,
I'll open the curtains and
watch the lightning conduct
your hands.

FOR A LONG TIME, what is known as 'world literature' was lopsided, mainly because the inhabitants of places conquered by great imperial powers like England were taught that 'literature' was written elsewhere. Mostly by Europeans and sometimes the odd Russian and that, as Thomas Macaulay said, 'A single shelf of a good European library is worth the whole native literature of India and Arabia.'

Macaulay would probably be alarmed to hear that Rumi is possibly the best-selling poet in the western world today, and when he wrote those words, how was he to know that in 1913, the great Bengali poet Rabindranath Tagore would go on to become the first non-European to win the Nobel Prize for Literature.

I mention these two poets because both of them have had enormous influence on my own ideas about poetry – Rumi, whose work I was introduced to by my friend, the Egyptian writer Ali Darwish, and Tagore, whose gorgeous *Gitanjali* I discovered when I worked at my first job as a bookmobile librarian in Jamaica.

Rumi and Tagore are both poets who drew deeply from their local culture and both are adepts of the spiritual, who, as a character in a story written by V.S. Naipaul says, write poems that 'sing to all humanity'. If this sounds as if I'm about to take off on a rant about post-colonial literature, I want to assure you that I am not. I am trying to move past post-colonial; I am looking forward to the day post-colonial officially ends, so that something new can be made manifest.

But to go back to where I started, generations of people in places like what used to be called the British West Indies were taught that real literature was not something produced locally because that sort of writing would have no appeal to international audiences. Hence, we were encouraged to regard the poems of Robert Burns, written in deep Scots dialect, as 'great literature', and to trivialise the poems of Louise Bennett, who wrote in Jamaican dialect. For a good part of her life, Louise Bennett had to contend with the wrath of the gatekeepers of Jamaican society who claimed that, by writing in a language that most Jamaicans spoke, she was bringing about the collapse of, if not western civilisation, then certainly, West Indian civilisation.

But one of the unintended and happier results of this insult to local literature was that there are generations of West Indian writers who are entirely comfortable with the great books in that good European Library to which Macaulay referred. Great writers like Nobel Laureate Derek Walcott, who repeatedly emphasised his love for 'his canon', even as he produced some of the most excellent poems written in modern times, poems inspired by local Caribbean culture. Thanks to a number of gifted writers, including Walcott, the world has come to accept that great writing can and does come from places like the Caribbean.

I believe that, here, I should hazard a guess as to what exactly caused the (current) interest in world literature. Time maybe, and without a doubt, the tireless efforts of a few stubborn independent publishers like Jessica Huntley of Bogle-L'Ouverture Publications and the heroic John La Rose and his partner Sarah White, who started New Beacon Books in London for the sole purpose of publishing the works of African, Black British, Caribbean, Asian and African American writers, who were, as we Jamaicans say, 'less counted' by mainstream publishers.

New Beacon Books and the Race Today Collective also hosted the International Book Fair of Radical Black and Third World Books, a dynamic gathering of writers, artists and independent publishers who came from all over the world to the city of London in the mid- to late-1980s. Poetry readings and musical performances by international artists were a regular feature of these events, where the world-famous Jamaican British poet and social activist Linton Kwesi Johnson is rightly credited with introducing the world to extraordinary writers like the late Mikey Smith.

It is safe to say that the success of what was possibly the world's first Black book fair helped to convince some mainstream publishers to look again at the market for world literature.

For Keith Jarrett Rainmaker – Iowa City

World literature also owes a great debt to the pioneering efforts of Margaret Busby, whose publishing house, Allison and Busby, was a game-changer in the world of books. Her *Daughters of Africa*, which focused on Black women writers in the African diaspora, was published in conjunction with another great supporter of the written word, Candida Lacey, and helped to pave the way for the rise of a number of women writers who are now big names in world literature.

Gifted translators also played a major part in bringing about this change in attitude, as did the increased freedom of movement between once far-flung places.

In the USA, individuals like the poet and publisher Haki Madhubuti, through his Third World Press in Chicago, helped to raise the level of awareness about the richness of world literature.

But I believe that the Iowa International Writing Program has done more for world literature than any other organisation. It would probably take someone like Malcolm Gladwell to figure out just how many students were inspired to a love of world literature through exposure to the IWP: becoming authors, professors, publishers, journalists, agents, literary critics and avid readers spreading enthusiasm and appreciation for the works of writers from the wider world.

In 1983 I was fortunate to become the first Jamaican to participate in the IWP. This came about in part through the efforts of the then US Ambassador to Jamaica, Bill Hewitt, who was a long-time supporter of the programme and a personal friend of Paul Engle and Hualing Nieh Engle, beautiful dreamers both. One of the writers in the programme that year, who was making his first trip outside of Africa, was the Nigerian author Amos Tutuola, whose highly original work continues to have a significant impact on literature today. At his reading in Iowa City, he was given a rock-star welcome by a massive crowd of students and lovers of literature, even as some writers and critics in his own country were still dismissing his project as eccentric and primitive. His fans from Iowa proved to be on the winning side of history because his work has gone on to make such an indelible mark on the rest of the world that there is actually a character in the television series *Law and Order SVU* (Odafin Tutuola) named for him.

I was an early beneficiary of the IWP back in 1983, before the Berlin Wall came down, before Nelson Mandela walked out of prison and Apartheid ended, before the so-called Iron Curtain buckled under its own weight, before the Arab Spring, and before the USA elected their first Black president, Barack Obama. The IWP brings writers from all over the known world and sets them down amidst not alien corn but the golden corn of hospitality and enlightenment that gives nourishment to writers and artists who, at their best, feed and nourish the world.

25

People I'd like to meet

AS I GROW OLDER, the list of people I'd like to meet before I leave this earth gets shorter and shorter. Some of the people I most love and admire have gone ahead so there is now no chance I'll meet them here below. All things considered, I've done pretty well in the meeting-of-important-people department. I will refrain from providing a full list here, but I will mention that I met Fidel Castro twice, and Archbishop Desmond Tutu once personally thanked me for reading some of my poems, as did Ahmed Kathrada, for whom I read at a function hosted for him by Professor Nesha Haniff in the Department of African and African American Studies at the University of Michigan. I once went to a small dinner where Harry Belafonte was the guest of honour, and Toni Morrison once chatted amiably with me at a gathering at the University of Toronto. I have spent time, on more than one occasion, in the company of Wole Soyinka, and Bob Marley used to nod to me like a mandarin whenever we passed each other on the streets of Kingston.

When Nelson Mandela died, I cried as much as I did on the day he was released from prison. That is to say, I bawled. Although my husband Ted and I once had the good fortune to sit one table away from him at a dinner at the Vergelegen Estate in South Africa, I never did actually meet him.

I did, however, meet Winnie Mandela, and I read her my poem 'Bedspread' (p.35) which I wrote for her. She cried openly and said that she'd been hearing about my poem for years, but she'd had no way of getting hold of it because she was a banned person. Then she hugged me very tightly for what seemed like a long time. After that hug I somehow felt much stronger, as if she had managed to transmit some of her enormous courage and fearlessness to me. That was one of the highlights of my life.

I always wanted to meet Muhammad Ali, I never did, and I know that a light went out in the world when he died. I felt the same when Seamus Heaney went home, after telling us not to be afraid. '*Noli timere,*' he told his wife, and I believe he meant it for all of us. I was beyond sad. But I did meet him just once in person, and I can honestly say that as people go he was one of the sweetest souls that I have ever encountered. I only mention him because I had always hoped to meet him again.

I once shared a stage with Maya Angelou. Hers was an extraordinary presence. I am glad I met her because I think she was perhaps one of the wisest people who ever lived. Something she said once in an interview has helped me to make sense of my own life, with its hard and sometimes frantic questing to find the 'one' with whom I could build a life. To paraphrase: Maya Angelou said that she no longer answered questions about her romantic relationships and marriages; that she went into every one of them with all the right appetites for what makes such unions work, they did not, and she chose to keep on moving. But, said she, there are people who elect to remain in dead relationships who somehow think that their decision to stay entombed in this way, gives them the right to look down on others who do not. I learned from her that I am not under any obligation to explain anything to anybody about my somewhat ramshackle romantic track record.

I wish I'd met Zora Neale Hurston in person. My dear, dear old friend Ivy Coverley who spent time in Zora's company told me that the great writer had a ball when she visited Jamaica in 1939, and that her stay had been greatly enhanced by the ministrations of a particularly good-looking Jamaican man and a fair measure of fine Jamaican rum. I also heard from Edna Manley that, during that same visit, she'd taken Zora to a Pocomania meeting in Jones Town. Mrs Manley said that things had been going really well up until a fight broke out at a political meeting that was taking place near the Poco yard. When the stone throwing between rival political factions started they had no choice but to run. So, Zora Neale Hurston and Edna Manley ran. They raced through the streets whooping and laughing like two wild young girls, laughing in the face of danger, loving all the excitement as they sprinted through the dark streets of West Kingston back up to the Manleys' palatial residence at Drumblair.

And it was only after they were safely home and had settled in to have a few drinks, that Edna remembered that she had driven them to the meeting, and that her car was still back there parked outside the Poco shepherd's yard.

And then there is the other woman writer whose work I admire greatly and whom I'd always hoped to meet. I remember feeling really pleased when I received an invitation to a luncheon in her honour, but once our eyes made four, as Jamaicans say, I could tell she was not happy to see me, and during the course of that lunch she sent out enough signals for me to know that she really did not want me around.

Now this could, in some weird way, have been regarded as a compliment, because the fact that one of the world's most successful writers was actually sufficiently aware of my work, to the extent that she could be all but be cutting her eye after me and saying things like 'All flowers are NOT roses,' which could only mean that she had read, or read about, my poem 'To Us, All Flowers are Roses'. I guess if ever I am interviewed by someone who asks, 'When did you realise that your work was well-known?' I could say, 'When x took issue with the title of one of my poems.'

But after that meeting, I decided that I no longer want to keep a list of people I'd like to meet. I'll just see who comes along and stay open to being surprised by joy.

Original Sources and Permissions

My grateful thanks to Evan Jones for his kind permission to quote extensively from 'The Song of the Banana Man'.

In 'Some poems that made me', the quote from 'The Port of Many Ships' is by permission of the Society of Authors as the Literary Representative of the Estate of John Masefield. The lines from 'A Careful Passion' by the wonderful Derek Walcott are quoted by very kind permission of his daughters Anna and Lizzie Walcott.

The 'Nadine Gordimer Memorial Lecture' was delivered at the 5th African Women Writers Symposium as part of Arts Alive International Festival, Johannesburg, South Africa, 2017. With thanks to Roshnie Moonsammy. Published in City Press, South Africa and Carcanet Blog.

'Redemption is the Key' was commissioned for the 2014 International Forum on the Novel, Villa Gillet, Lyon, France.

'Immortal, Invisible, God Only Wise' was specially commissioned by editor/poet Jeffrey Johnson for 'Stars Shall bend Their Voices', Poets, Favourite Hymns and Spiritual Songs, forthcoming from Orison Books.

'The Caribbean imaginary' is adapted from a talk given at NYU.

'My Painted Skirt Like A Scenic 78' first appeared in PALAVER magazine, edited by Michael Jarrett.

'For Derek Walcott' was published in Review 95: Literature and Arts of the Americas edited by Dan Shapiro.

'For Keith Jarrett Rainmaker' is adapted from a talk given at 50th Anniversary of International Writing Programme, Iowa City, Iowa.

Acknowledgements

To my son Miles, with love. All day all night.

To my brothers, Keith, Karl, Kingsley, Howard and Nigel, for all their kindness and support over these many years.

Sincere thanks to Hugh Hodges for being such a good friend and generous reader of my work.

To Margaret Busby, Candida Lacey, Dawn Sackett, Lydia Cooper and Linda McQueen for making this book into a book.

To Swithin Wilmot for information on Redemption Ground Market.

To Asif Khan, for the author photo taken with his phone!

To Edward Baugh and Hilary Beckles of the U.W.I. Mona.

To Michael Schmidt and Carcanet for all they do for my poems.

To Petrona Morrison, Errol Moo Young and Tony Robinson for over forty years of friendship.

To Donna Singh, who told me thirty years ago that I should write a book of essays.

To Ted, for always believing in this work.

About the author

LORNA GOODISON is the Poet Laureate of Jamaica, and a major figure in world literature. Her many awards include the Commonwealth Poetry Prize, the Musgrave Gold Medal from Jamaica, one of Canada's largest literary prizes for *From Harvey River: A Memoir of My Mother and Her People*, and the Windham Campbell Prize for Poetry from Yale University. She has published three collections of short stories, including *By Love Possessed*, and ten collections of poetry. Her *Collected Poems* was published in 2017. She is Professor Emerita at University of Michigan, where she was the Lemuel A. Johnson Professor of English and African and Afroamerican Studies.